Epistles: first Series

by

Swami Vivekananda

Double9 BOOKS

Epistles: first Series
by Swami Vivekananda

ISBN: 978-93-59393-41-4

Published by

DOUBLE 9 BOOKS
2/13-B, Ansari Road
Daryaganj, New Delhi – 110002
info@double9books.com
www.double9books.com
Tel. 011-40042856

ABOUT THE AUTHOR

Swami Vivekananda was born Narendranath Datta in India on January 12, 1863. He died on July 4, 1902, and was the most important student of the Indian saint Ramakrishna. He was an important part of bringing Vedanta and Yoga to the West. He is also charged with making people more aware of other religions and making Hinduism a major world religion. Vivekananda had a lot of success at the Parliament. In the years that followed, he gave hundreds of lectures across the United States, England, and Europe to spread the main ideas of Hinduism. He also started the Vedanta Society of New York and the Vedanta Society of San Francisco, which is now the Vedanta Society of Northern California. Both of these groups became the basis for Vedanta Societies in the West. Vivekananda was one of the most important philosophers and social reformers in India at the time. He was also one of the most successful and powerful Vedanta missionaries in the West.People now think of him as one of the most important people in modern India and Hinduism. Mahatma Gandhi said that after reading Vivekananda's works, he loved his country a thousand times more.

CONTENTS

I 11

II 12

III 14

IV 19

V 26

VI 31

VII 33

VIII 36

IX 38

X 39

XI 41

XII 43

XIII 45

XIV 48

XV 50

XVI 51

XVII 52

XVIII 53

XIX 55

XX 56

XXI 57

XXII 59

XXIII 61

XXIV 62
XXV 63
XXVI 65
XXVII 66
XXVIII 69
XXIX 70
XXX 72
XXXI 74
XXXII 76
XXXIII 79
XXXIV 80
XXXV 81
XXXVI 82
XXXVII 84
XXXVIII 85
XXXIX 86
XL 90
XLI 91
XLII 92
XLIII 93
XLIV 95
XLV 96
XLVI 98
XLVII 99
XLVIII 100
XLIX 101
L 102
LI 103
LII 104
LIII 106

LIV....................107
LV....................108
LVI....................110
LVII....................111
LVIII....................114
LIX....................116
LX....................117
LXI....................118
LXII....................120
LXIII....................121
LXIV....................122
LXV....................124
LXVI....................125
LXVII....................127
LXVIII....................129
LXIX....................132
LXX....................133
LXXI....................134
LXXII....................135
LXXIII....................137
LXXIV....................138
LXXV....................141
LXXVI....................144
LXXVII....................145
LXXVIII....................147
LXXIX....................150
LXXX....................151
LXXXI....................152
LXXXII....................153
LXXXIII....................154

LXXXIV 155
LXXXV 156
LXXXVI 157
LXXXVII 158
LXXXVIII 159
LXXXIX 160
XC 163
XCI 164
XCII 165
XCIII 166
XCIV 167
XCV 169
XCVI 170
XCVII 171
XCVIII 172
XCIX 173
C 174
CI 175
CII 177
CIII 178
CIV 180
CV 181
CVI 183
CVII 184
CVIII 185
CIX 187
CX 188
CXI 190
CXII 191
CXIII 192

CXIV 193
CXV 195
CXVI 197
CXVII...198
CXVIII 199
CXIX 200
CXX 201
CXXI 202
CXXII...203
CXXIII 204

I

(Translated from Bengali)

ALLAHABAD
5th January, 1890.

MY DEAR FAKIR, (Shri Yajneshwar Bhattacharya)

. . . A word for you. Remember always, I may not see you again. Be moral. Be brave. Be a heart-whole man. Strictly moral, brave unto desperation. Don't bother your head with religious theories. Cowards only sin, brave men never, no, not even in mind. Try to love anybody and everybody. Be a *man* and try to make those immediately under your care, namely Ram, Krishnamayi, and Indu, brave, moral, and sympathising. No religion for you, my children, but morality and bravery. No cowardice, no sin, no crime, no weakness — the rest will come of itself. . . . And don't take Ram with you ever or ever allow him to visit a theatre or any enervating entertainment whatever.

Yours affectionately,

VIVEKANANDA.

MY DEAR RAM, KRISHNAMAYI, AND INDU,

Bear in mind, my children, that only cowards and those who are weak commit sin and tell lies. The brave are always moral. Try to be moral, try to be brave, try to be sympathising.

Yours,

VIVEKANANDA.

II

BOMBAY,
20th September, 1892.

DEAR PANDITJI MAHÂRÂJ, (Pandit Shankarlal of Khetri.)

Your letter has reached me duly. I do not know why I should be undeservingly praised. "None is good, save One, that is, God", as the Lord Jesus hath said. The rest are only tools in His hands. "Gloria in Excelsis", "Glory unto God in the highest", and unto men that deserve, but not to such an undeserving one like me. Here "the servant is *not* worthy of the hire"; and a Fakir, especially, has no right to any praise whatsoever, for would you praise your servant for simply doing his duty?

. . . My unbounded gratitude to Pandit Sundarlalji, and to my Professor (With whom he read the Mahâ-Bhâshya on Pânini.) for this kind remembrance of me.

Now I would tell you something else. The Hindu mind was ever deductive and never synthetic or inductive. In all our philosophies, we always find hair-splitting arguments, taking for granted some general proposition, but the proposition itself may be as childish as possible. Nobody ever asked or searched the truth of these general propositions. Therefore independent thought we have almost none to speak of, and hence the dearth of those sciences which are the results of observation and generalization. And why was it thus? — From two causes: The tremendous heat of the climate forcing us to love rest and contemplation better than activity, and the Brâhmins as priests never undertaking journeys or voyages to distant lands. There were voyagers and people who travelled far; but they were almost always traders, i.e. people from whom priestcraft and their own sole love for gain had taken away all capacity for intellectual development. So their observations, instead of adding to the store of human knowledge, rather degenerated it; for their observations were bad and their accounts exaggerated and tortured into fantastical shapes, until they passed all recognition.

So you see, we must travel, we must go to foreign parts. We must see how the engine of society works in other countries, and keep free and open communication with what is going on in the minds of other nations, if we really want to be a nation again. And over and above all, we must cease to tyrannise. To what a ludicrous state are we brought! If a Bhângi comes to anybody as a Bhangi, he would be shunned as the plague; but no sooner does he get a cupful of water poured upon his head with some mutterings of prayers by a Pâdri, and get a coat on his back, no matter how threadbare, and come into the room of the most orthodox Hindu — I don't see the man who then dare refuse him a chair and a hearty shake of the hands! Irony can go no further. And come and see what they, the Pâdris, are doing here in the Dakshin (south). They are converting the lower classes by lakhs; and in Travancore, the most priestridden country in India — where every bit of land is owned by the Brahmins . . . nearly one-fourth has become Christian! And I cannot blame them; what part have they in David and what in Jesse? When, when, O Lords shall man be brother to man?

Yours,

VIVEKANANDA.

III

ORIENTAL HOTEL
YOKOHAMA.
10th July, 1893.

DEAR ALASINGA, BALAJI, G. G., BANKING CORPORATION, AND ALL MY MADRAS FRIENDS,

Excuse my not keeping you constantly informed of my movements. One is so busy every day, and especially myself who am quite new to the life of possessing things and taking care of them. That consumes so much of my energy. It is really an awful botheration.

From Bombay we reached Colombo. Our steamer remained in port for nearly the whole day, and we took the opportunity of getting off to have a look at the town. We drove through the streets, and the only thing I remember was a temple in which was a very gigantic Murti (image) of the Lord Buddha in a reclining posture, entering Nirvâna....

The next station was Penang, which is only a strip of land along the sea in the body of the Malaya Peninsula. The Malayas are all Mohammedans and in old days were noted pirates and quite a dread to merchantmen. But now the leviathan guns of modern turreted battleships have forced the Malayas to look about for more peaceful pursuits. On our way from Penang to Singapore, we had glimpses of Sumatra with its high mountains, and the Captain pointed out to me several places as the favourite haunts of pirates in days gone by. Singapore is the capital of the Straits Settlements. It has a fine botanical garden with the most splendid collection of palms. The beautiful fan-like palm, called the traveller's palm, grows here in abundance, and the bread-fruit tree everywhere. The celebrated mangosteen is as plentiful here as mangoes in Madras, but mango is nonpareil. The people here are not half so dark as the people of Madras, although so near the line. Singapore possesses a fine museum too.

Hong Kong next. You feel that you have reached China, the Chinese element predominates so much. All labour, all trade seems to be in their hands. And Hong Kong is real China. As soon as the steamer casts anchor, you are besieged with hundreds of Chinese boats to carry you to the land.

These boats with two helms are rather peculiar. The boatman lives in the boat with his family. Almost always, the wife is at the helms, managing one with her hands and the other with one of her feet. And in ninety per cent of cases, you find a baby tied to her back, with the hands and feet of the little Chin left free. It is a quaint sight to see the little John Chinaman dangling very quietly from his mother's back, whilst she is now setting with might and main, now pushing heavy loads, or jumping with wonderful agility from boat to boat. And there is such a rush of boats and steamlaunches coming in and going out. Baby John is every moment put into the risk of having his little head pulverised, pigtail and all; but he does not care a fig. This busy life seems to have no charm for him, and he is quite content to learn the anatomy of a bit of rice-cake given to him from time to time by the madly busy mother. The Chinese child is quite a philosopher and calmly goes to work at an age when your Indian boy can hardly crawl on all fours. He has learnt the philosophy of necessity too well. Their extreme poverty is one of the causes why the Chinese and the Indians have remained in a state of mummified civilisation. To an ordinary Hindu or Chinese, everyday necessity is too hideous to allow him to think of anything else.

Hong Kong is a very beautiful town. It is built on the slopes of hills and on the tops too, which are much cooler than the city. There is an almost perpendicular tramway going to the top of the hill, dragged by wire-rope and steam-power.

We remained three days at Hong Kong and went to see Canton, which is eighty miles up a river. The river is broad enough to allow the biggest steamers to pass through. A number of Chinese steamers ply between Hong Kong and Canton. We took passage on one of these in the evening and reached Canton early in the morning. What a scene of bustle and life! What an immense number of boats almost covering the waters! And not only those that are carrying on the trade, but hundreds of others which serve as houses to live in. And quite a lot of them so nice and big! In fact, they are big houses two or three storeys high, with verandahs running round and streets between, and all floating!

We landed on a strip of ground given by the Chinese Government to foreigners to live in. Around us on both sides of the river for miles and miles is the big city — a wilderness of human beings, pushing, struggling, surging, roaring. But with all its population, all its activity, it is the dirtiest town I saw, not in the sense in which a town is called dirty in India, for as to that not a speck of filth is allowed by the Chinese to go waste; but because of the Chinaman, who has, it seems, taken a vow never to bathe! Every house is a shop, people living only on the top floor. The streets are very very narrow, so that you almost touch the shops on both sides as you pass. At every ten paces you find meat-stalls, and there are shops which sell cat's and dog's meat. Of course, only the poorest classes of Chinamen eat dog or cat.

The Chinese ladies can never be seen. They have got as strict a zenana as the Hindus of Northern India; only the women of the labouring classes can be seen. Even amongst these, one sees now and then a woman with feet smaller than those of your youngest child, and of course they cannot be said to walk, but hobble.

I went to see several Chinese temples. The biggest in Canton is dedicated to the memory of the first Buddhistic Emperor and the five hundred first disciples of Buddhism. The central figure is of course Buddha, and next beneath Him is seated the Emperor, and ranging on both sides are the statues of the disciples, all beautifully carved out of wood.

From Canton I returned back to Hong Kong, and from thence to Japan. The first port we touched was Nagasaki. We landed for a few hours and drove through the town. What a contrast! The Japanese are one of the cleanliest peoples on earth. Everything is neat and tidy. Their streets are nearly all broad, straight, and regularly paved. Their little houses are cage-like, and their pine-covered evergreen little hills form the background of almost every town and village. The short-statured, fair-skinned, quaintly-dressed Japs, their movements, attitudes, gestures, everything is picturesque. Japan is the land of the picturesque! Almost every house has a garden at the back, very nicely laid out according to Japanese fashion with small shrubs, grass-plots, small artificial waters, and small stone bridges.

From Nagasaki to Kobe. Here I gave up the steamer and took the land-route to Yokohama, with a view to see the interior of Japan.

I have seen three big cities in the interior — Osaka, a great manufacturing town, Kyoto, the former capital, and Tokyo, the present capital. Tokyo is nearly twice the size of Calcutta with nearly double the population.

No foreigner is allowed to travel in the interior without a passport.

The Japanese seem now to have fully awakened themselves to the necessity of the present times. They have now a thoroughly organised army equipped with guns which one of their own officers has invented and which is said to be second to none. Then, they are continually increasing their navy. I have seen a tunnel nearly a mile long, bored by a Japanese engineer.

The match factories are simply a sight to see, and they are bent upon making everything they want in their own country. There is a Japanese line of steamers plying between China and Japan, which shortly intends running between Bombay and Yokohama.

I saw quite a lot of temples. In every temple there are some Sanskrit Mantras written in Old Bengali characters. Only a few of the priests know Sanskrit. But they are an intelligent sect. The modern rage for progress has penetrated even the priesthood. I cannot write what I have in my mind about the Japs in one short letter. Only I want that numbers of our young men should pay a visit to Japan and China every year. Especially to the Japanese, India is still the dreamland of everything high and good. And you, what are you? . . . talking twaddle all your lives, vain talkers, what are you? Come, see these people, and then go and hide your faces in shame. A race of dotards, you lose your caste if you come out! Sitting down these hundreds of years with an ever-increasing load of crystallised superstition on your heads, for hundreds of years spending all your energy upon discussing the touchableness or untouchableness of this food or that, with all humanity crushed out of you by the continuous social tyranny of ages — what are you? And what are you doing now? . . . promenading the sea-shores with books in your hands — repeating undigested stray bits of European brainwork, and the whole soul bent upon getting a thirty-rupee clerkship, or at best becoming a lawyer — the height of young India's ambition — and every student with a whole brood of hungry children cackling at his heels and asking for bread! Is there not water enough in the sea to drown you, books, gowns, university diplomas, and all?

Come, be men! Kick out the priests who are always against progress, because they would never mend, their hearts would never become big. They are the offspring of centuries of superstition and tyranny. Root out priest craft first. Come, be men! Come out of your narrow holes and have a look abroad. See how nations are on the march! Do you love man? Do you love your country? Then come, let us struggle for higher and better things; look not back, no, not even if you see the dearest and nearest cry. Look not back, but forward!

India wants the sacrifice of at least a thousand or her young men — men, mind, and not brutes. The English Government has been the instrument, brought over here by the Lord, to break your crystallised civilisation, and

Madras supplied the first men who helped in giving the English a footing. How many men, unselfish, thorough-going men, is Madras ready now to supply, to struggle unto life and death to bring about a new state of things sympathy for the poor, and bread to their hungry mouths, enlightenment to the people at large — and struggle unto death to make men of them who have been brought to the level of beasts, by the tyranny of your forefathers?

Yours etc.,

VIVEKANANDA.

PS. Calm and silent and steady work, and no newspaper humbug, no name-making, you must always remember.

V.

IV

BREEZY MEADOWS,
METCALF, MASS.,
20th August, 1893.

DEAR ALASINGA,

Received your letter yesterday. Perhaps you have by this time got my letter from Japan. From Japan I reached Vancouver. The way was by the Northern Pacific. It was very cold and I suffered much for want of warm clothing. However, I reached Vancouver anyhow, and thence went through Canada to Chicago. I remained about twelve days in Chicago. And almost every day I used to go to the Fair. It is a tremendous affair. One must take at least ten days to go through it. The lady to whom Varada Rao introduced me and her husband belong to the highest Chicago society, and they were so very kind to me. I took my departure from Chicago and came to Boston. Mr. Lâlubhâi was with me up to Boston. He was very kind to me. . . .

The expense I am bound to run into here is awful. You remember, you gave me £170 in notes and £9 in cash. It has come down to £130 in all!! On an average it costs me £1 every day; a cigar costs eight annas of our money. The Americans are so rich that they spend money like water, and by forced legislation keep up the price of everything so high that no other nation on earth can approach it. Every common coolie earns nine or ten rupees a day and spends as much. All those rosy ideas we had before starting have melted, and I have now to fight against impossibilities. A hundred times I had a mind to go out of the country and go back to India. But I am determined, and I have a call from Above; I see no way, but His eyes see. And I must stick to my guns, life or death. . . .

Just now I am living as the guest of an old lady in a village near Boston. I accidentally made her acquaintance in the railway train, and she invited me to come over and live with her. I have an advantage in living with her, in saving for some time my expenditure of £1 per day, and she has the advantage of inviting her friends over here and showing them a curio from India! And all this must be borne. Starvation, cold, hooting in the streets on account of my quaint dress, these are what I have to fight against. But, my dear boy, no great things were ever done without great labour.

. . . Know, then, that this is the land of Christians, and any other influence than that is almost zero. Nor do I care a bit for the enmity of any — ists in the world. I am here amongst the children of the Son of Mary and the Lord Jesus will help me. They like much the broad views of Hinduism and my love for the Prophet of Nazareth. I tell them that I preach nothing against the Great One of Galilee. I only ask the Christians to take in the Great Ones of Ind along with the Lord Jesus, and they appreciate it.

Winter is approaching and I shall have to get all sorts of warm clothing, and we require more warm clothing than the natives. . . Look sharp, my boy, take courage. We are destined by the Lord to do great things in India. Have faith. We will do. We, the poor and the despised, who really feel, and not those. . . .

In Chicago, the other day, a funny thing happened The Raja of Kapurthala was here, and he was being lionised by some portion of Chicago society. I once met the Raja in the Fair grounds, but he was too big to speak with a poor Fakir. There was an eccentric Mahratta Brâhmin selling nail-made pictures in the Fair, dressed in a dhoti. This fellow told the reporters all sorts of things against the Raja —, that he was a man of low caste, that those Rajas were nothing but slaves, and that they generally led immoral lives, etc., etc. And these truthful (?) editors, for which America is famous, wanted to give to the boy's stories some weight; and so the next day they wrote huge columns in their papers about the description of a man of wisdom from India, meaning me — extolling me to the skies, and putting all sorts of words in my mouth, which I never even dreamt of, and ascribing to me all those remarks made by the Mahratta Brahmin about the Raja of Kapurthala. And it was such a good brushing that Chicago society gave up the Raja in hot haste. . . . These newspaper editors made capital out of me to give my countryman a brushing. That shows, however, that in this country intellect carries more weight than all the pomp of money and title.

Yesterday Mrs. Johnson, the lady superintendent of the women's prison, was here. They don't call it prison but reformatory here. It is the grandest thing I have seen in America. How the inmates are benevolently treated, how they are reformed and sent back as useful members of society; how grand, how beautiful, You must see to believe! And, oh, how my heart ached to think of what we think of the poor, the low, in India. They have no chance, no escape, no way to climb up. The poor, the low, the sinner in India have no friends, no help — they cannot rise, try however they may. They sink lower and lower every day, they feel the blows showered upon them by a cruel society, and they do not know whence the blow comes. They have forgotten that they too are men. And the result is slavery. Thoughtful people within the last few years have seen it, but unfortunately laid it at the door of the Hindu religion, and to them, the only way of bettering is by crushing this grandest religion of the world. Hear me, my friend, I have discovered the secret through the grace of the Lord. Religion is not in fault. On the other hand, your religion teaches you that every being is only your own self multiplied. But it was the want of practical application, the want of sympathy — the want of heart. The Lord once more came to you as Buddha and taught you how to feel, how to sympathise with the poor, the miserable, the sinner, but you heard Him not. Your priests invented the horrible story that the Lord was here for deluding demons with false doctrines! True indeed, but we are the demons, not those that believed. And just as the Jews denied the Lord Jesus and are since that day wandering over the world as homeless beggars, tyrannised over by everybody, so you are bond-slaves to any nation that thinks it worth while to rule over you. Ah, tyrants! you do not know that the obverse is tyranny, and the reverse slavery. The slave and the tyrant are synonymous.

Balaji and G. G. may remember one evening at Pondicherry — we were discussing the matter of sea-voyage with a Pandit, and I shall always remember his brutal gestures and his Kadâpi Na (never)! They do not know that India is a very small part of the world, and the whole world looks down with contempt upon the three hundred millions of earthworms crawling upon the fair soil of India and trying to oppress each other. This state of things must be removed, not by destroying religion but by following the great teachings of the Hindu faith, and joining with it the wonderful sympathy of that logical development of Hinduism — Buddhism.

A hundred thousand men and women, fired with the zeal of holiness, fortified with eternal faith in the Lord, and nerved to lion's courage by their sympathy for the poor and the fallen and the downtrodden, will go over the length and breadth of the land, preaching the gospel of salvation, the gospel of help, the gospel of social raising-up — the gospel of equality.

No religion on earth preaches the dignity of humanity in such a lofty strain as Hinduism, and no religion on earth treads upon the necks of the poor and the low in such a fashion as Hinduism. The Lord has shown me that religion is not in fault, but it is the Pharisees and Sadducees in Hinduism, hypocrites, who invent all sorts of engines of tyranny in the shape of doctrines of Pâramârthika and Vyâvahârika.

Despair not; remember the Lord says in the Gita, "To work you have the right, but not to the result." Gird up your loins, my boy. I am called by the Lord for this. I have been dragged through a whole life full of crosses and tortures, I have seen the nearest and dearest die, almost of starvation; I have been ridiculed, distrusted, and have suffered for my sympathy for the very men who scoff and scorn. Well, my boy, this is the school of misery, which is also the school for great souls and prophets for the cultivation of sympathy, of patience, and, above all, of an indomitable iron will which quakes not even if the universe be pulverised at our feet. I pity them. It is not their fault. They are children, yea, veritable children, though they be great and high in society. Their eyes see nothing beyond their little horizon of a few yards — the routine-work, eating, drinking, earning, and begetting, following each other in mathematical precision. They know nothing beyond — happy little souls! Their sleep is never disturbed, their nice little brown studies of lives never rudely shocked by the wail of woe, of misery, of degradation, and poverty, that has filled the Indian atmosphere — the result of centuries of oppression. They little dream of the ages of tyranny, mental, moral, and physical, that has reduced the image of God to a mere beast of burden; the emblem of the Divine Mother, to a slave to bear children; and life itself, a curse. But there are others who see, feel, and shed tears of blood in their hearts, who think that there is a remedy for it, and who are ready to apply this remedy at any cost, even to the giving up of life. And "of such is the kingdom of Heaven". Is it not then natural, my friends, that they have no time to look down from their heights to the vagariese of these contemptible little insects, ready every moment to spit their little venoms?

Trust not to the so-called rich, they are more dead than alive. The hope lies in you — in the meek, the lowly, but the faithful. Have faith in the Lord; no policy, it is nothing. Feel for the miserable and look up for help — it *shall come.* I have travelled twelve years with this load in my heart and this idea in my head. I have gone from door to door of the so-called rich and great. With a bleeding heart I have crossed half the world to this strange land, seeking for help. The Lord is great. I know He will help me. I may perish of cold or hunger in this land, but I bequeath to you, young men, this sympathy, this struggle for the poor, the ignorant, the oppressed. Go now this minute to the temple of Pârthasârathi, (Shri Krishna as Sârathi, charioteer, of Pârtha or Arjuna.) and before Him who was friend to the poor and lowly cowherds of Gokula, who never shrank to embrace the Pariah Guhaka, who accepted the invitation of a prostitute in preference to that of the nobles and saved her in His incarnation as Buddha — yea, down on your faces before Him, and make a great sacrifice, the sacrifice of a whole life for them, for whom He comes from time to time, whom He loves above all, the poor, the lowly, the oppressed. Vow, then, to devote your whole lives to the cause of the redemption of these three hundred millions, going down and down every day.

It is not the work of a day, and the path is full of the most deadly thorns. But Parthasarathi is ready to be our Sârathi — we know that. And in His name and with eternal faith in Him, set fire to the mountain of misery that has been heaped upon India for ages — and it shall be burned down. Come then, look it in the face, brethren, it is a grand task, and we are so low. But we are the sons of Light and children of God. Glory unto the Lord, we will succeed. Hundreds will fall in the struggle, hundreds will be ready to take it up. I may die here unsuccessful, another will take up the task. You know the disease, you know the remedy, only have faith. Do not look up to the so-called rich and great; do not care for the heartless intellectual writers, and their cold-blooded newspaper articles. Faith, sympathy — fiery faith and fiery sympathy! Life is nothing, death is nothing, hunger nothing, cold nothing. Glory unto the Lord — march on, the Lord is our General. Do not look back to see who falls — forward — onward! Thus and thus we shall go on, brethren. One falls, and another takes up the work.

From this village I am going to Boston tomorrow. I am going to speak at a big Ladies' Club here, which is helping Ramâbâi. I must first go and buy some clothing in Boston. If I am to live longer here, my quaint dress will not do. People gather by hundreds in the streets to see me. So what I want is to dress myself in a long black coat, and keep a red robe and turban to wear when I lecture. This is what the ladies advise me to do, and they are the rulers here, and I must have their sympathy. Before you get this letter my money would come down to somewhat about £70 of £60. So try your best to send some money. It is necessary to remain here for some time to have any influence here. I could not see the phonograph for Mr. Bhattacharya as I got his letter here. If I go to Chicago again, I will look for them. I do not know whether I shall go back to Chicago or not. My friends there write me to represent India. And the gentleman, to whom Varada Rao introduced me, is one of the directors of the Fair; but then I refused as I would have to spend all any little stock of money in remaining more than a month in Chicago.

In America, there are no classes in the railway except in Canada. So I have to travel first-class, as that is the only class; but I do not venture in the Pullmans. They are very comfortable — you sleep, eat, drink, even bathe in them, just as if you were in a hotel — but they are too expensive.

It is very hard work getting into society and making yourself heard. Now nobody is in the towns, they are all away in summer places. They will all come back in winter. Therefore I must wait. After such a struggle, I am not going to give up easily. Only try your best to help me as much as you can; and even if you cannot, I must try to the end. And even if I die of cold or disease or hunger here, you take up the task. Holiness sincerity, and faith. I have left instructions with Cooks to forward any letter or money to me wherever I am. Rome was not built in a day. If you can keep me here for six months at least, I hope everything will come right. In the meantime I am trying my best to find any plank I can float upon. And if I find out any means to support myself, I shall wire to you immediately.

First I will try in America; and if I fail, try in England; if I fail, go back to India and wait for further commands from High. Ramdas's father has gone to England. He is in a hurry to gone home. He is a very good man at heart, only the Baniya roughness on the surface. It would take more than twenty days for the letter to reach. Even now it is so cold in New England that every day we have fires night and morning. Canada is still colder. I never saw snow on such low hills as there.

Gradually I can make my way; but that means a longer residence in this horribly expensive country. Just now the raising of the Rupee in India has created a panic in this country, and lots of mills have been stopped. So I cannot hope for anything just now, but I must wait.

Just now I have been to the tailor and ordered some winter clothings, and that would cost at least Rs. 300 and up. And still it would not be good clothes, only decent. Ladies here are very particular about a man's dress, and they are the power in this country. They. . . never fail the missionaries. They are helping our Ramabai every year. If you fail in keeping me here, send some money to get me out of the country. In the meantime if anything turns out in my favour, I will write or wire. A word costs Rs. 4 in cable!!

Yours,

VIVEKANANDA.

V

CHICAGO,
2nd November, 1893.

DEAR ALASINGA,

I am so sorry that a moment's weakness on my part should cause you so much trouble; I was out of pocket at that time. Since then the Lord sent me friends. At a village near Boston I made the acquaintance of Dr. Wright, Professor of Greek in the Harvard University. He sympathised with me very much and urged upon me the necessity of going to the Parliament of Religions, which he thought would give me an introduction to the nation. As I was not acquainted with anybody, the Professor undertook to arrange everything for me, and eventually I came back to Chicago. Here I, together with the oriental and occidental delegates to the Parliament of Religions, were all lodged in the house of a gentleman.

On the morning of the opening of the Parliament, we all assembled in a building called the Art Palace, where one huge and other smaller temporary halls were erected for the sittings of the Parliament. Men from all nations were there. From India were Mazoomdar of the Brâhmo Samâj, and Nagarkar of Bombay, Mr. Gandhi representing the Jains, and Mr. Chakravarti representing Theosophy with Mrs. Annie Besant. Of these, Mazoomdar and I were, of course, old friends, and Chakravarti knew me by name. There was a grand procession, and we were all marshalled on to the platform. Imagine a hall below and a huge gallery above, packed with six or seven thousand men and women representing the best culture of the country, and on the platform learned men of all the nations of the earth. And I, who never spoke in public in my life, to address this august assemblage!! It was opened in great form with music and ceremony and speeches; then the delegates were introduced one by one, and they stepped up and spoke. Of course my heart was fluttering, and my tongue nearly dried up; I was so nervous and could not venture to speak in the morning. Mazoomdar made a nice speech, Chakravarti a nicer one, and they were much applauded.

They were all prepared and came with ready-made speeches. I was a fool and had none, but bowed down to Devi Sarasvati and stepped up, and Dr. Barrows introduced me. I made a short speech. I addressed the assembly as "Sisters and Brothers of America", a deafening applause of two minutes followed, and then I proceeded; and when it was finished, I sat down, almost exhausted with emotion. The next day all the papers announced that my speech was the hit of the day, and I became known to the whole of America. Truly has it been said by the great commentator Shridhara — "

मूकं करोति वाचालं

— Who maketh the dumb a fluent speaker." His name be praised! From that day I became a celebrity, and the day I read my paper on Hinduism, the hall was packed as it had never been before. I quote to you from one of the papers: "Ladies, ladies, ladies packing every place — filling every corner, they patiently waited and waited while the papers that separated them from Vivekananda were read", etc. You would be astonished if I sent over to you the newspaper cuttings, but you already know that I am a hater of celebrity. Suffice it to say, that whenever I went on the platform, a deafening applause would be raised for me. Nearly all the papers paid high tributes to me, and even the most bigoted had to admit that "This man with his handsome face and magnetic presence and wonderful oratory is the most prominent figure in the Parliament", etc., etc. Sufficient for you to know that never before did an Oriental make such an impression on American society.

And how to speak of their kindness? I have no more wants now, I am well off, and all the money that I require to visit Europe I shall get from here. . . . A boy called Narasimhâchârya has cropped up in our midst. He has been loafing about the city for the last three years. Loafing or no loafing, I like him; but please write to me all about him if you know anything. He knows you. He came in the year of the Paris Exhibition to Europe. . . .

I am now out of want. Many of the handsomest houses in this city are open to me. All the time I am living as a guest of somebody or other. There is a curiosity in this nation, such as you meet with nowhere else. They want to know everything, and their women — they are the most advanced in the world. The average American woman is far more cultivated than the average American man. The men slave all their life for money, and the women snatch every opportunity to improve themselves. And they are a very kind-hearted, frank people. Everybody who has a fad to preach comes here, and I am sorry to say that most of these are not sound. The Americans have their faults too, and what nation has not? But this is my summing up: Asia laid the germs of civilization, Europe developed man, and America is developing the woman and the masses. It is the paradise of the woman and the labourer. Now contrast the American masses and women with ours, and you get the idea at once. The Americans are fast becoming liberal. Judge them not by the specimens of *hard-shelled Christians* (it is their own phrase) that you see in India. There are those here too, but their number is decreasing rapidly, and this great nation is progressing fast towards that spirituality which is the standard boast of the Hindu.

The Hindu must not give up his religion, but must keep religion within its proper limits end give freedom to society to grow. All the reformers in India made the serious mistake of holding religion accountable for all the horrors of priestcraft and degeneration and went forth with to pull down the indestructible structure, and what was the result? Failure! Beginning from Buddha down to Ram Mohan Roy, everyone made the mistake of holding caste to be a religious institution and tried to pull down religion and caste all together, and failed. But in spite of all the ravings of the priests, caste is simply a crystallised social institution, which after doing its service is now filling the atmosphere of India with its stench, and it can only be removed by giving back to the people their lost social individuality. Every man born here knows that he is a *man*. Every man born in India knows that he is a slave of society. Now, freedom is the only condition of growth; take that off, the result is degeneration. With the introduction of modern competition, see how caste is disappearing fast! No religion is now necessary to kill it. The Brâhmana shopkeeper, shoemaker, and wine-distiller are common in Northern India. And why? Because of competition. No man is prohibited from doing anything he pleases for his livelihood under the present Government, and the result is neck and neck competition, and thus thousands are seeking and finding the highest level they were born for, instead of vegetating at the bottom.

I must remain in this country at least through the winter, and then go to Europe. The Lord will provide everything for me. You need not disturb yourself about it. I cannot express my gratitude for your love.

Day by day I am feeling that the Lord is with me, and I am trying to follow His direction. His will be done. . . . We will do great things for the world, and that for the sake of doing good and not for name and fame.

"Ours not to reason why, ours but to do and die." Be of good cheer and believe that we are selected by the Lord to do great things, and we will do them. Hold yourself in readiness, i.e. be pure and holy, and love for love's sake. Love the poor, the miserable, the downtrodden, and the Lord will bless you.

See the Raja of Ramnad and others from time to time and urge them to sympathise with the masses of India. Tell them how they are standing on the neck of the poor, and that they are not fit to be called men if they do not try to raise them up. Be fearless, the Lord is with you, and He will yet raise the starving and ignorant millions of India. A railway porter here is better educated than many of your young men and most of your princes. Every American woman has far better education than can be conceived of by the majority of Hindu women. Why cannot we have the same education? We must.

Think not that you are poor; money is not power, but goodness, holiness. Come and see how it is so all over the world.

Yours with blessings,

VIVEKANANDA.

PS. By the bye, your uncle's paper was the most curious phenomenon I ever saw. It was like a tradesman's catalogue, and it was not thought fit to be read in the Parliament. So Narasimhacharya read a few extracts from it in a side hall, and nobody understood a word of it. Do not tell him of it. It is a great art to press the largest amount of thought into the smallest number of words. Even Manilal Dvivedi's paper had to be cut very short. More than a thousand papers were read, and there was no time to give to such wild perorations. I had a good long time given to me over the ordinary half hour, . . . because the most popular speakers were always put down last, to hold the audience. And Lord bless them, what sympathy they have, and what patience! They would sit from ten o'clock in the morning to ten o'clock at night — only a recess of half an hour for a meal, and paper after paper read, most of them very trivial, but they would wait and wait to hear their favourites.

Dharmapâla of Ceylon was one of the favourites But unfortunately he was not a good speaker. He had only quotations from Max Müller and Rhys Davids to give them. He is a very sweet man, and we became very intimate during the Parliament.

A Christian lady from Poona, Miss Sorabji, and the Jain representative, Mr. Gandhi, are going to remain longer in the country end make lecture tours. I hope they will succeed. Lecturing is a very profitable occupation in this country and sometimes pays well.

Mr. Ingersoll gets five to six hundred dollars a lecture. He is the most celebrated lecturer in this country. Do not publish this letter. After reading, send it to the Maharaja (of Khetri). I have sent him my photograph in America.

V

VI

(Translated from Bengali)

C/O GEORGE W. HALE ESQ.,
541 DEARBORN AVENUE, CHICAGO,
28th December, 1893.

DEAR HARIPADA, (Haripada Mitra)

It is very strange that news of my Chicago lectures has appeared in the Indian papers; for whatever I do, I try my best to avoid publicity. Many things strike me here. It may be fairly said that there is no poverty in this country. I have never seen women elsewhere as cultured and educated as they are here. Well-educated men there are in our country, but you will scarcely find anywhere women like those here. It is indeed true, that "the Goddess Herself lives in the houses of virtuous men as Lakshmi". I have seen thousands of women here whose hearts are as pure and stainless as snow. Oh, how free they are! It is they who control social and civic duties Schools and colleges are full of women, and in our country women cannot be safely allowed to walk in the streets! Their kindness to me is immeasurable. Since I came here, I have been welcomed by them to their houses. They are providing me with food, arranging for my lectures, taking me to market, and doing everything for my comfort and convenience. I shall never be able to repay in the least the deep debt of gratitude I owe to them.

Do you know who is the real "Shakti-worshipper"? It is he who knows that God is the omnipresent force in the universe and sees in women the manifestation of that Force. Many men here look upon their women in this light. Manu, again, has said that gods bless those families where women are happy and well treated. Here men treat their women as well as can be desired, and hence they are so prosperous, so learned, so free, and so energetic. But why is it that we are slavish, miserable, and dead? The answer is obvious.

And how pure and chaste are they here! Few women are married before twenty or twenty-five, and they are as free as the birds in the air. They go to market, school, and college, earn money, and do all kinds of work. Those who are well-to-do devote themselves to doing good to the poor. And what are we doing? We are very regular in marrying our girls at eleven years of age lest they should become corrupt and immoral. What does our Manu enjoin? "Daughters should be supported and educated with as much care and attention as the sons." As sons should be married after observing Brahmacharya up to the thirtieth year, so daughters also must observe Brahmacharya and be educated by their parents. But what are we actually doing? Can you better the condition of your women? Then there will be hope for your well-being. Otherwise you will remain as backward as you are now.

If anybody is born of a low caste in our country, he is gone for ever, there is no hope for him. Why? What a tyranny it is! There are possibilities, opportunities, and hope for every individual in this country. Today he is poor, tomorrow he may become rich and learned and respected. Here everyone is anxious to help the poor. In India there is a howling cry that we are very poor, but how many charitable associations are there for the well-being of the poor? How many people really weep for the sorrows and sufferings of the millions of poor in India? Are we *men*? What are we doing for their livelihood, for their improvement? We do not touch them, we avoid their company! Are we men? Those thousands of Brâhmanas — what are they doing for the low, downtrodden masses of India? "Don't touch", "Don't touch", is the only phrase that plays upon their lips! How mean and degraded has our eternal religion become at their hands! Wherein does our religion lie now? In "Don't-touchism" alone, and nowhere else!

I came to this country not to satisfy my curiosity, nor for name or fame, but to see if I could find any means for the support of the poor in India. If God helps me, you will know gradually what those means are.

As regards spirituality, the Americans are far inferior to us, but their society is far superior to ours. We will teach them our spirituality and assimilate what is best in their society.

With love and best wishes,

Yours,

VIVEKANANDA.

VII

C/O GEORGE W. HALE ESQ.,
541 DEARBORN AVENUE, CHICAGO,
24th January, 1894.

DEAR FRIENDS, (His disciples in Madras)

Your letters have reached me. I am surprised that so much about me has reached you. The criticism you mention of the *Interior* is not to be taken as the attitude of the American people. That paper is almost unknown here, and belongs to what they call a "blue-nose Presbyterian paper", very bigoted. Still all the "blue-noses" are not ungentlemanly. The American people, and many of the clergy, are very hospitable to me. That paper wanted a little notoriety by attacking a man who was being lionised by society. That trick is well known here, and they do not think anything of it. Of course, our Indian missionaries may try to make capital out of it. If they do, tell them, "Mark, Jew, a judgment has come upon you!" Their old building is tottering to its foundation and must come down in spite of their hysterical shrieks. I pity them — if their means of living fine lives in India is cut down by the influx of oriental religions here. But not one of their leading clergy is ever against me. Well, when I am in the pond, I must bathe thoroughly.

I send you a newspaper cutting of the short sketch of our religion which I read before them. Most of my speeches are extempore. I hope to put them in book form before I leave the country. I do not require any help from India, I have plenty here. Employ the money you have in printing and publishing this short speech; and translating it into the vernaculars, throw it broadcast; that will keep us before the national mind. In the meantime do not forget our plan of a central college, and the starting from it to all directions in India. Work hard. . . .

About the women of America, I cannot express my gratitude for their kindness. Lord bless them. In this country, women are the life of every movement, and represent all the culture of the nation, for men are too busy to educate themselves.

I have received Kidi's letters. With the question whether caste shall go or come I have nothing to do. My idea is to bring to the door of the meanest, the poorest, the noble ideas that the human race has developed both in and out of India, and let them think for themselves. Whether there should be caste or not, whether women should be perfectly free or not, does not concern me. "Liberty of thought and action is the only condition of life, of growth and well-being." Where it does not exist, the man, the race, the nation must go down.

Caste or no caste, creed or no creed, any man, or class, or caste, or nation, or institution which bars the power of free thought and action of an individual — even so long as that power does not injure others — is devilish and must go down.

My whole ambition in life is to set in motion a machinery which will bring noble ideas to the door of everybody, and then let men and women settle their own fate. Let them know what our forefathers as well as other nations have thought on the most momentous questions of life. Let them see specially what others are doing now, and then decide. We are to put the chemicals together, the crystallization will be done by nature according to her laws. Work hard, be steady, and have faith in the Lord. Set to work, I am coming sooner or later. Keep the motto before you — "Elevation of the masses without injuring their religion".

Remember that the nation lives in the cottage. But, alas! nobody ever did anything for them. Our modern reformers are very busy about widow remarriage. Of course, I am a sympathiser in every reform, but the fate of a nation does not depend upon the number of husbands their widows get, but upon the *condition of the masses*. Can you raise them? Can you give them back their lost individuality without making them lose their innate spiritual nature? Can you become an occidental of occidentals in your spirit of equality, freedom, work, and energy, and at the same time a Hindu to the very backbone in religious culture and instincts? This is to be done and *we will do it*. You are all *born to do it*. Have faith in yourselves, great convictions are the mothers of great deeds. Onward for ever! Sympathy for the poor, the downtrodden, even unto death — this is our motto.

Onward, brave lads!

Yours affectionately,

VIVEKANANDA.

IX

U. S. A.,
20th May, 1894.

MY DEAR SHARAT (SARADANANDA),

I am in receipt of your letter and am glad to learn that Shashi (Ramakrishnananda) is all right. Now I tell you a curious fact. Whenever anyone of you is sick, let him himself or anyone of you visualise him in your mind, and mentally say and strongly imagine that he is all right. That will cure him quickly. You can do it even without his knowledge, and even with thousands of miles between you. Remember it and do not be ill any more. You have received the money by this time. If you all like, you can give to Gopal Rs. 300/- from the amount I sent for the Math. I have no more to send now. I have to look after Madras now.

I cannot understand why Sanyal is so miserable on account of his daughters' marriage. After all, he is going to drag his daughters through the dirty Samsâra (world) which he himself wants to escape! I can have but one opinion of that — condemnation! I hate the very name of marriage, in regard to a boy or a girl. Do you mean to say that I have to help in putting someone into bondage, you fool! If my brother Mohin marries, I will throw him off. I am very decided about that. . . .

Yours in love,

VIVEKANANDA.

PS. Do not publish this letter; but there is no harm in preaching the idea of elevating the masses by means of a central college, and bringing education as well as religion to the door of the poor by means of missionaries trained in this college. Try to interest everybody.

I send you a few newspaper cuttings — only from the very best and highest. The one by Dr. Thomas is very valuable as written by one of the, if not the leading clergymen of America. The *Interior* with all its fanaticism and thirst for notoriety was bound to say that I was the public favourite. I cut a few lines from that magazine also.

V.

VIII

NEW YORK,
9th April, 1894.

DEAR ALASINGA,

I got your last letter a few days ago. You see I am so very busy here, and have to write so many letters every day, that you cannot expect frequent communications from me. But I try my best to keep you in touch with whatever is going on here. I will write to Chicago for one of the books on the Parliament of Religions to be sent over to you. But by this time you have got two of my short speeches.

Secretary Saheb writes me that I must come back to India, because that is my field. No doubt of that. But my brother, we are to light a torch which will shed a lustre over all India. So let us not be in a hurry; everything will come by the grace of the Lord. I have lectured in many of the big towns of America, and have got enough to pay my passage back after paying the awful expenses here. I have made a good many friends here, some of them very influential. Of course, the orthodox clergymen are against me; and seeing that it is not easy to grapple with me, they try to hinder, abuse, and vilify me in every way; and Mazoomdar has come to their help. He must have gone mad with jealousy. He has told them that I was a big fraud, and a rogue! And again in Calcutta he is telling them that I am leading a most sinful life in America, specially unchaste! Lord bless him! My brother, no good thing can be done without obstruction. It is only those who persevere to the end that succeed. . . . I believe that the Satya Yuga (Golden Age) will come when there will be one caste, one Veda, and peace and harmony. This idea of Satya Yuga is what would revivify India. Believe it. One thing is to be done if you can do it. Can you convene a big meeting in Madras, getting Ramnad or any such big fellow as the President, and pass a resolution of your entire satisfaction at my representation of Hinduism here, and send it to the *Chicago Herald*, *Inter-Ocean*, and the *New York Sun*, and the *Commercial Advertiser* of Detroit (Michigan). Chicago is in Illinois. *New York Sun* requires no particulars. Detroit is in the State of Michigan. Send copies to Dr. Barrows, Chairman of the Parliament of Religions, Chicago. I have

forgotten his number, but the street is Indiana Avenue. One copy t
J. Bagley of Detroit, Washington Ave.

Try to make this meeting as big as possible. Get hold of all the b
who must join it for their religion and country. Try to get a letter f
Mysore Maharaja and the Dewan approving the meeting and its pu
so of Khetri — in fact, as big and noisy a crowd as you can.

The resolution would be of such a nature that the Hindu com
of Madras, who sent me over, expressing its entire satisfaction in n
here etc.

Now try if it is possible. This is not much work. Get also l
sympathy from all parts you can and print them and send copie
American papers — as quickly as you can. That will go a long
brethren. The B— S— fellows here are trying to talk all sorts of n
We must stop their mouths as fast as we can.

Up boys, and put yourselves to the task! If you can do that, I
we will be able to do much in future. Old Hinduism for ever! Down
liars and rogues! Up, up, my boys, we are sure to win!

As to publishing my letters, such parts as ought to be publish
be published for our friends till I come. When once we begin to
shall have a tremendous "boom", but I do not want to talk without
I do not know, but G. C. Ghosh and Mr. Mitra of Calcutta can g
the sympathisers of my late Gurudeva to do the same in Calcutt
can, so much the better. Ask them, if they can, to pass the same res
in Calcutta. There are thousands in Calcutta who sympathise
movement. However I have more faith in you than in them.

Nothing more to write.

Convey my greetings to all our friends — for whom I am always

Yours with b

VIVEKAN

X

CHICAGO,
28th May, 1894.

DEAR ALASINGA,

I could not reply to your note earlier, because I was whirling to and fro from New York to Boston, and also I awaited Narasimha's letter. I do not know when I am going back to India. It is better to leave everything in the hands of Him who is at my back directing me. Try to work without me, as if I never existed. Do not wait for anybody or anything. Do whatever you can. Build your hope on none. Before writing about myself, I will tell you about Narasimha. He has proved a complete failure. . . . However he wrote to me for help in the last stage, and I will try to help him as much as is in my power. Meanwhile you tell his people to send money as soon as they can for him to go over. . . . He is in distress. Of course I will see that he does not starve.

I have done a good deal of lecturing here.... The expenses here are terrible; money has to fly, although I have been almost always taken care of everywhere by the nicest and the highest families.

I do not know whether I shall go away this summer or not. Most probably not. In the meantime try to organise and push on our plans. Believe you can do everything. Know that the Lord is with us, and so, onward, brave souls!

I have had enough appreciation in my own country. Appreciation or no appreciation, sleep not, slacken not. You must remember that not a bit even of our plans has been as yet carried out.

Act on the educated young men, bring them together, and organise them. Great things can be done by great sacrifices only. No selfishness, no name, no fame, yours or mine, nor my Master's even! Work, work the idea, the plan, my boys, my brave, noble, good souls — to the wheel, to the wheel put your shoulders! Stop not to look back for name, or fame, or any such nonsense. Throw self overboard and work. Remember, "The grass when made into a rope by being joined together can even chain a mad elephant." The Lord's blessings on you all! His power be in you all— as I believe it is *already*. "Wake up, stop not until the goal is reached", say the Vedas. Up, up, the long night is passing, the day is approaching, the wave has risen, nothing will be able to resist its tidal fury. The spirit, my boys, the spirit; the love, my children, the love; the faith, the belief; and fear not! The greatest sin is fear.

My blessings on all. Tell all the noble souls in Madras who have helped our cause that I send them my eternal love and gratitude, but I beg of them not to slacken. Throw the idea broadcast. Do not be proud; do not insist upon anything dogmatic; do not go against anything — ours is to put chemicals together, the Lord knows how and when the crystal will form. Above all, be not inflated with my success or yours. Great works are to be done; what is this small success in comparison with what is to come? Believe, believe, the decree has gone forth, the fiat of the Lord has gone forth — India must rise, the masses and the poor are to be made happy. Rejoice that you are the chosen instruments in His hands. The flood of spirituality has risen. I see it is rolling over the land resistless, boundless, all-absorbing. Every man to the fore, every good will be added to its forces, every hand will smooth its way, and glory be unto the Lord! . . .

I do not require any help. Try to get up a fund, buy some magic-lanterns, maps, globes, etc., and some chemicals. Get every evening a crowd of the poor and low, even the Pariahs, and lecture to them about religion first, and then teach them through the magic-lantern and other things, astronomy, geography, etc., in the dialect of the people. Train up a band of fiery young men. Put your fire in them and gradually increase the organization, letting it widen and widen its circle. Do the best you can, do not wait to cross the river when the water has all run down. Printing magazines, papers, etc., are good, no doubt, but actual work, my boys even if infinitesimal, is better than eternal scribbling and talking. Call a meeting at Bhattacharya's. Get a little money and buy those things I have just now stated, hire a hut, and go to work. Magazines are secondary, but this is primary. You must have a hold on the masses. Do not be afraid of a small beginning, great things come afterwards. Be courageous. Do not try to lead your brethren, but serve them. The brutal mania for leading has sunk many a great ship in the waters of life. Take care especially of that, i.e. be unselfish even unto death, and work. I could not write all I was going to say, but the Lord will give you all understanding, my brave boys. At it, my boys! Glory unto the Lord! . . .

Yours affectionately,

VIVEKANANDA.

XI

U. S. A.,
11th July, 1894.

DEAR ALASINGA,

You must never write to me anywhere else but 541 Dearborn Ave., Chicago. Your last letter has travelled the whole country to come to me, and this was only because I am so well known. Some of the resolutions are to be sent to Dr. Barrows with a letter thanking him for his kindness to me and asking him to publish the letter in some American newspapers — as that would be the best refutation of the false charges of the missionaries that I do not represent anybody. Learn business, my boy. We will do great things yet! Last year I only sowed the seeds; this year I mean to reap. In the meanwhile, keep up as much enthusiasm as possible in India. Let Kidi go his own way. He will come out all right in time. I have taken his responsibility. He has a perfect right to his own opinion. Make him write for the paper; that will keep him in good temper! My blessings on him.

Start the journal and I will send you articles from time to time. You must send a paper and a letter to Professor J. H. Wright of Harvard University, Boston, thanking him as having been the first man who stood as my friend and asking him to publish it in the papers, thus giving the lie to the missionaries.

In the Detroit lecture I got $900, i.e. Rs. 2,700. In other lectures, I earned in one, $2,500, i.e. Rs. 7,500 in one hour, but got only 200 dollars! I was cheated by a roguish Lecture Bureau. I have given them up. I spent a good deal here; only about $3,000 remains.

I shall have to print much matter next year. I am going regularly to work. . . . The sheer power of the *will* will do everything. . . . You must organise a society which should regularly meet, and write to me about it as often as you can. In fact, get up as much enthusiasm as you can. Only, *beware* of falsehood. Go to work, my boys, the fire will come to you! The faculty of organisation is entirely absent in our nature, but this has to be infused. The great secret is — absence of jealousy. Be always ready to concede to the opinions of your brethren, and try always to conciliate. That is the whole secret. Fight on bravely! Life is short! Give it up to a great cause. Why do you not write anything about Narasimha? He is almost starving. I gave him something. Then he went over to somewhere, I do not know where, and does not write. Akshaya is a good boy. I like him very much. No use quarrelling with the Theosophists. Do not go and tell them all I write to you. . . . Theosophists are our pioneers, do you know? Now Judge is a Hindu and Col. a Buddhist, and Judge is the ablest man here. Now tell the Hindu Theosophists to support Judge. Even if you can write Judge a letter, thanking him as a co-religionist and for his labours in presenting Hinduism before Americans; that will do his heart much good. We must not join any sect, but we must sympathise and work with each. . . . Work, work — conquer all by your love! . . .

Try to expand. Remember the *only sign of life* is motion and growth. You must send the passed resolution to Dr. J. H. Barrows. . ., Dr. Paul Carus. . ., Senator Palmer. . ., Mrs. J. J. Bagley. . ., it must come officially. . . . I write this because I do not think you know the ways of foreign nations. . . . Keep on steadily. So far we have done wonderful things. Onward, brave souls, we will gain! Organise and found societies and go to work, that is the only way.

At this time of the year there is not much lecturing to be done here; so I will devote myself to my pen and write. I shall be hard at work all the time, and then, when the cold weather comes and people return to their homes, I shall begin lecturing again and at the same time organise societies.

My love and blessings to you all. I never forget anybody, though I do not write often. Then again, I am now, continuously travelling, and letters have to be redirected from one place to another.

Work hard. Be holy and pure and the fire will come.

Yours affectionately,

VIVEKANANDA.

XII

ANNISQUAM,
20th August, 1894.

DEAR SISTER, (Isabelle McKindley)

Your very kind letter duly reached me at Annisquam. I am with the Bagleys once more. They are kind as usual. Professor Wright was not here. But he came day before yesterday and we have very nice time together. Mr. Bradley of Evanston, whom you have met at Evanston, was here. His sister-in-law had me sit for a picture several days and had painted me. I had some very fine boating and one evening overturned the boat and had a good drenching — clothes and all.

I had very very nice time at Greenacre. They were all so earnest and kind people. Fanny Hartley and Mrs. Mills have by this time gone back home I suppose.

From here I think I will go back to New York. Or I may go to Boston to Mrs. Ole Bull. Perhaps you have heard of Mr. Ole Bull, the great violinist of this country. She is his widow. She is a very spiritual lady. She lives in Cambridge and has a fine big parlour made of woodwork brought all the way from India. She wants me to come over to her any time and use her parlour to lecture. Boston of course is the great field for everything, but the Boston people as quickly take hold of anything as give it up; while the New Yorkers are slow, but when they get hold of anything they do it with a mortal grip.

I have kept pretty good health all the time and hope to do in the future. I had no occasion yet to draw on my reserve, yet I am rolling on pretty fair. And I have given up all money-making schemes and will be quite satisfied with a bite and a shed and work on.

I believe you are enjoying your summer retreat. Kindly convey my best regards and love to Miss Howe and Mr. Frank Howe.

Perhaps I did not tell you in my last how I slept and lived and preached under the trees and for a few days at least found myself once more in the atmosphere of heaven.

Most probably I will make New York my centre for the next winter; and as soon as I fix on that, I will write to you. I am not yet settled in my ideas of remaining in this country any more. I cannot settle anything of that sort. I must bide my time. May the Lord bless you all for ever and ever is the constant prayer of your ever affectionate brother,

VIVEKANANDA.

XIII

U. S. A.,
31st August, 1894.

DEAR ALASINGA,

I just now saw an editorial on me about the circular from Madras in the *Boston Transcript*. Nothing has reached me yet. They will reach me soon if you have sent them already. So far you have done wonderfully, my boy. Do not mind what I write in some moments of nervousness. One gets nervous sometimes alone in a country 15,000 miles from home, having to fight every inch of ground with orthodox inimical Christians. You must take those into consideration, my brave boy, and work right along.

Perhaps you have heard from Bhattacharya that I received a beautiful letter from G. G. His address was scrawled in such a fashion as to become perfectly illegible to me. So I could not reply to him direct. But I have done all that he desired. I have sent over my photograph and written to the Raja of Mysore. Now I have sent a phonograph to Khetri Raja. . . .

Now send always Indian newspapers about me to me over here. I want to read them in the papers themselves — do you know? Now lastly, you must write to me all about Mr. Charu Chandra who has been so kind to me. Give him my heartfelt thanks; but (between you and me) I unfortunately do not remember him. Would you give me particulars?

The Theosophists here now like me, but they are 650 in all!! There are the Christian Scientists. All of them like me. They are about a million. I work with both, but join none, and will with the Lord's grace would them both after the true fashion; for they are after all mumbling half realised truth. Narasimha, perhaps, by the time this reaches you, will get the money etc.

I have received a letter from *Cat*, but it requires a book to answer all his queries. So I send him my blessings through you and ask you to remind him that we agree to differ — and see the harmony of contrary points. So it does not matter what he believes in; he must act. Give my love to Balaji, G. G., Kidi, Doctor, and to all our friends and all the great and patriotic souls, who were brave and noble enough to sink their differences for their country's cause.

With a magazine or journal or organ — you become the Secretary thereof. You calculate the cost of starting the magazine and the work, how much the least is necessary to start it, and then write to me giving name and address of the Society, and I will send you money myself, and not only that, I will get others in America to subscribe annually to it liberally. So ask them of Calcutta to do the same. Give me Dharmapala's address. He is a great and good man. He will work wonderfully with us. Now organise a little society. You will have to take charge of the whole movement, not as a *leader*, but as a *servant*. Do you know, the least show of leading destroys everything by rousing jealousy?

Accede to everything. Only try to retain all of my friends together. Do you see? And work slowly up. Let G. G. and others, who have no immediate necessity for earning something, do as they are doing, i.e. casting the idea broadcast. G. G. is doing well at Mysore. That is the way. Mysore will be in time a great stronghold.

I am now going to write my *mems* in a book and *next* winter will go about this country organising *societies* here. This is a great field of work, and everything done here prepares *England*. So far you have done very well indeed, my brave boy — all strength shall be given to you.

I have now Rs. 9,000 with me, part of which I will send over to you for the organisation; and I will get many people to send money to you in Madras yearly, half-yearly, or monthly. You now start a Society and a journal and the necessary apparatus. This must be a secret amongst only a few — but at the same time try to collect funds from Mysore and elsewhere to build a temple in Madras which should have a library and some rooms for the office and the preachers who should be Sannyâsins, and for Vairâgis (men of renunciation) who may chance to come. Thus we shall progress inch by inch. This is a great field for my work, and everything done here prepares the way for my coming work in England. . . .

You know the greatest difficulty with me is to keep or even to touch money. It is disgusting and debasing. So you must organise a Society to take charge of the practical and pecuniary part of it. I have friends here who take care of all my monetary concerns. Do you see? It will be a wonderful relief to me to get rid of horrid money affairs. So the sooner you organise yourselves and you be ready as secretary and treasurer to enter into direct communication with my friends and sympathisers here, the better for you and me. Do that quickly, and write to me. Give the society a non-sectarian name. . . Do you write to my brethren at the Math to organise in a similar fashion. . . . Great things are in store for you Alasinga. Or if you think proper, you get some of the big folks to be named as office-bearers of the

Society, while you work in the real sense. Their name will be a great thing. If your duties are too severe and do not let you have any time, let G. G. do the business part, and by and by I hope to make you independent of your college work so that you may, without starving yourself and family, devote your whole soul to the work. So work, my boys, work! The rough part of the work has been smoothened and rounded; now it will roll on better and better every year. And if you can simply keep it going well until I come to India, the work will progress by leaps and bounds. Rejoice that you have done so much. When you feel gloomy, think what has been done within the last year. How, rising from nothing, we have the eyes of the world fixed upon us now. Not only India, but the world outside, is expecting great things of us. Missionaries or M — or foolish officials — none will be able to resist truth and love and sincerity. Are you sincere? unselfish even unto death? and loving? Then fear not, not even death. Onward, my lads! The whole world requires Light. It is expectant! India alone has that Light, not in magic, mummery, and charlatanism, but in the teaching of the glories of the spirit of real religion — of the highest spiritual truth. That is why the Lord has preserved the race through all its vicissitudes unto the present day. Now the time has come. Have faith that you are all, my brave lads, born to do great things! Let not the barks of puppies frighten you — no, not even the thunderbolts of heaven — but stand up and work!

Ever yours affectionately,

VIVEKANANDA.

XIV

U. S. A.,
21st September, 1894.

DEAR ALASINGA,

. . . I have been continuously travelling from place to place and working incessantly, giving lectures, holding classes, etc.

I have not been able to write yet for my proposed book. Perhaps I may be able to take it in hand later on. I have made some nice friends here amongst the liberal people, and a few amongst the orthodox. I hope to return soon to India — I have had enough of this country and especially as too much work is making me nervous. The giving of too many public lectures and constant hurry have brought on this nervousness. I do not care for this busy, meaningless, money-making life. So you see, I will soon return. Of course, there is a growing section with whom I am very popular, and who will like to have me here all the time. But I think I have had enough of newspaper blazoning and humbugging of a public life. I do not care the least for it. . . .

There is no hope for money for our project here. It is useless to hope. No large number of men in any country do good out of mere sympathy. The few who really give money in the Christian lands often do so through priestcraft and fear of hell. So it is as in our Bengali proverb, "Kill a cow and make a pair of shoes out of the leather and give them in charity to a Brahmana". So it is here, and so everywhere; and then, the Westerners are miserly in comparison to our race. I sincerely believe that the Asians are the most charitable race in the world, only they are very poor.

I am going to live for a few months in New York. That city is the head, hand, and purse of the country. Of course, Boston is called the Brahmanical city, and here in America there are hundreds of thousands that sympathise with me. . . . The New York people are very open. I will see what can be done there, as I have some very influential friends. After all, I am getting disgusted with this lecturing business. It will take a long time for the Westerners to understand the higher spirituality, Everything is £. s. d. to them. If a religion brings them money or health or beauty or long life, they will all flock to it, otherwise not. . . .

Give to Balaji, G. G., and all of our friends my best love.

Yours with everlasting love,

VIVEKANANDA.

XV

U. S. A.,
21st September, 1894.

DEAR KIDI,

I am very sorry to hear your determination of giving up the world so soon. The fruit falls from the tree when it gets ripe. So wait for the time to come. Do not hurry. Moreover, no one has the right to make others miserable by his foolish acts. Wait, have patience, everything will come right in time.

Yours with blessings,

VIVEKANANDA.

XVI

BOSTON,
26th Sept, 1894.

DEAR SISTER, (Isabelle McKindley)

Your letter with the India mail just to hand. A quantity of newspaper clippings were sent over to me from India. I send them back for your perusal and safe keeping.

I am busy writing letters to India last few days. I will remain a few days more in Boston.

With my love and blessings,

Yours ever affly.,
VIVEKANANDA.

XVII

U. S. A.
27th September, 1894.

DEAR ALASINGA,

. . . One thing I find in the books of my speeches and sayings published in Calcutta. Some of them are printed in such a way as to savour of political views; whereas I am no politician or political agitator. I care only for the Spirit — when that is right everything will be righted by itself.... So you must warn the Calcutta people that no political significance be ever attached falsely to any of my writings or sayings. What nonsense I . . . I heard that Rev. Kali Charan Banerji in a lecture to Christian missionaries said that I was a political delegate. If it was said publicly, then publicly ask the Babu for me to write to any of the Calcutta papers and prove it, or else take back his foolish assertion. This is their trick! I have said a few harsh words in honest criticism of Christian governments in general, but that does not mean that I care for, or have any connection with politics or that sort of thing. Those who think it very grand to print extracts from those lectures and want to prove that I am a political preacher, to them I say, "Save me from my friends." . . .

. . . Tell my friends that a uniform silence is all my answer to my detractors. If I give them tit for tat, it would bring us down to a level with them. Tell them that truth will take care of itself, and that they are not to fight anybody for me. They have much to learn yet, and they are only children. They are still full of foolish golden dreams — mere boys!

. . .This nonsense of public life and newspaper blazoning has disgusted me thoroughly. I long to go back to the Himalayan quiet.

Ever yours affectionately,

VIVEKANANDA.

XVIII

U. S. A.,
29th September, 1894.

DEAR ALASINGA,

You all have done well, my brave unselfish children. I am so proud of you. . . . Hope and do not despair. After such a start, if you despair you are a fool. . . .

Our field is India, and the value of foreign appreciation is in rousing India up. That is all. . . . We must have a strong base from which to spread. . . . Do not for a moment quail. Everything will come all right. It is will that moves the world.

You need not be sorry, my son, on account of the young men becoming Christians. What else can they be under the existing social bandages, especially in Madras? Liberty is the first condition of growth. Your ancestors gave every liberty to the soul, and religion grew. They put the body under every bondage, and society did not grow. The opposite is the case in the West — every liberty to society, none to religion. Now are falling off the shackles from the feet of Eastern society as from those of Western religion.

Each again will have its type; the religious or introspective in India, the scientific or out-seeing in the West. The West wants every bit of spirituality through social improvement. The East wants every bit of social power through spirituality. Thus it was that the modern reformers saw no way to reform but by first crushing out the religion of India. They tried, and they failed. Why? Because few of them ever studied their own religion, and not *one* ever *underwent* the training necessary to understand the *Mother of all religions*. I claim that no destruction of religion is necessary to improve the Hindu society, and that this state of society exists not on account of religion, but because religion has not been applied to society as it should have been. This I am ready to prove from our old books, every word of it. This is what I teach, and this is what we must struggle all our lives to carry out. But it will take time, a long time to study. Have patience and work.

उद्धरेदात्मनात्मानम्

— Save yourself by yourself.

Yours etc.,

VIVEKANANDA.

PS. The present Hindu society is organised only for spiritual men, and hopelessly crushes out everybody else. Why? Where shall they go who want to enjoy the world a little with its frivolities? Just as our religion takes in all, so should our society. This is to be worked out by first understanding the true principles of our religion and then applying them to society. This is the slow but sure work to be done.

V.

XIX

WASHINGTON,
23rd October, 1894.

DEAR VEHEMIA CHAND LIMBDI,

I am going on very well in this country. By this time I have become one of their own teachers. They all like me and my teachings.... I travel all over the country from one place to another, as was my habit in India, preaching and teaching. Thousands and thousands have listened to me and taken my ideas in a very kindly spirit. It is the most expensive country, but the Lord provides for me everywhere I go.

With my love to you and all my friends there (Limbdi, Rajputana).

Yours,

VIVEKANANDA.

XX

WASHINGTON,
C/O MRS. T. TOTTEN.
1708 W I STREET,
26th (?) *October, 1894.*

DEAR SISTER, (Isabelle McKindley)

Excuse my long silence; but I have been regularly writing to Mother Church. I am sure you are all enjoying this nice cool weather. I am enjoying Baltimore and Washington very much. I will go hence to Philadelphia. I thought Miss Mary was in Philadelphia, and so I wanted her address. But as she is in some other place near Philadelphia, I do not want to give her the trouble to come up to see me, as Mother Church says.

The lady with whom I am staying is Mrs. Totten, a niece of Miss Howe. I will be her guest more than a week yet; so you may write to me to her care.

I intend going over to England this winter somewhere in January or February. A lady from London with whom one of my friends is staying has sent an invitation to me to go over as her guest; and from India they are urging me every day to come back.

How did you like Pitoo in the cartoon? Do not show it to anybody. It is too bad of our people to caricature Pitoo that way.

I long ever so much to hear from you, but take a little more care to make your letter just a bit more distinct. Do not be angry for the suggestion.

Your ever loving brother,

VIVEKANANDA.

XXI

WASHINGTON,
27th October, 1894.

BLESSED AND BELOVED, (Alasinga Perumal)

By this time you must have received my other letters. You must excuse me for certain harshness of tone sometimes, and you know full well how I love you. You have asked me often to send over to you all about my movements in this country and all my lecture reports. I am doing exactly here what I used to do in India. Always depending on the Lord and making no plans ahead.... Moreover you must remember that I have to work incessantly in this country, and that I have no time to put together my thoughts in the form of a book, so much so, that this constant rush has worn my nerves, and I am feeling it. I cannot express my obligation to you, G. G., and all my friends in Madras, for the most unselfish and heroic work you did for me. But it was not at all meant to blazon me, but to make you conscious of your own strength. I am not an organiser, my nature tends towards scholarship and meditation. I think I have worked enough, now I want rest and to teach a little to those that have come to me from my Gurudeva (venerable Guru). You have known now what you can do, for it is really you, young men of Madras, that have done all; I am only the figurehead. I am a Tyâgi (detached) monk. I only want one thing. I do not believe in a God or religion which cannot wipe the widow's tears or bring a piece of bread to the orphan's mouth. However sublime be the theories, however well-spun may be the philosophy — I do not call it religion so long as it is confined to books and dogmas. The eye is in the forehead and not in the back. Move onward and carry into practice that which you are very proud to call your religion, and God bless you!

Look not at me, look to yourselves. I am happy to have been the occasion of rousing an enthusiasm. Take advantage of it, float along with it, and everything will come right. Love never fails, my son; today or tomorrow or ages after, truth will conquer. Love shall win the victory. Do you love your fellow men? Where should you go to seek for God — are not all the poor, the miserable, the weak, Gods? Why not worship them first? Why go to dig a well on the shores of the Gangâ? Believe in the omnipotent power of love. Who cares for these tinsel puffs of name? I never keep watch of what the newspapers are saying. Have you love? — You are omnipotent. Are you perfectly unselfish? If so, you are irresistible. It is character that pays everywhere. It is the Lord who protects His children in the depths of the sea. Your country requires heroes; be heroes! God bless you!

Everybody wants me to come over to India. They think we shall be able to do more if I come over. They are mistaken, my friend. The present enthusiasm is only a little patriotism, it means nothing. If it is true and genuine, you will find in a short time hundreds of heroes coming forward and carrying on the work. Therefore know that you have really done all, and go on. Look not for me. Akshoy Kumar Ghosh is in London. He sent a beautiful invitation from London to come to Miss Müller's. And I hope I am going in January or February next. Bhattacharya writes me to come over. Here is a grand field. What have I to do with this "ism" or that "ism"? I am the servant of the Lord, and where on earth is there a better field than here for propagating all high ideas? Here, where if one man is against me, a hundred hands are ready to help me; here, where man feels for man, weeps for his fellow-men and women are goddesses! Even idiots may stand up to hear themselves praised, and cowards assume the attitude of the brave when everything is sure to turn out well, but the true hero works in silence. How many Buddhas die before one finds expression! My son, I believe in God, and I believe in man. I believe in helping the miserable. I believe in going even to hell to save others. Talk of the Westerners? They have given me food, shelter, friendship, protection — even the most orthodox Christians! What do our people do when any of their priests go to India? You do not touch them even, they are MLECHCHHAS! No man, no nation, my son, can hate others and live; India's doom was sealed the very day they invented the word MLECHCHHA and stopped from communion with others. Take care how you foster that idea. It is good to talk glibly about the Vedanta, but how hard to carry out even its least precepts!

Ever yours with blessings,

VIVEKANANDA.

PS. Take care of these two things — love of power and jealousy. Cultivate always "faith in yourself".

XXII

U. S. A.,
30th November, 1894.

DEAR ALASINGA,

I am glad to leant that the phonograph and the letter have reached you safely. You need not send any more newspaper cuttings. I have been deluged with them. Enough of that. Now go to work for the organisation. I have started one already in New York and the Vice-President will soon write to you. Keep correspondence with them. Soon I hope to get up a few in other places. We must organise our forces not to make a sect — not on religious matters, but on the secular business part of it. A stirring propaganda must be launched out. Put your heads together and organise.

What nonsense about the miracle of Ramakrishna! . . .Miracles I do not know nor understand. Had Ramakrishna nothing to do in the world but turning wine into the Gupta's medicine? Lord save me from such Calcutta people! What materials to work with! If they can write a real life of Shri Ramakrishna with the idea of showing what he came to do and teach, let them do it, otherwise let them not distort his life and sayings. These people want to know God who see in Shri Ramakrishna nothing but jugglery! . . . Now let Kidi translate his love, his knowledge, his teachings, his eclecticism, etc. This is the theme. The life of Shri Ramakrishna was an extraordinary searchlight under whose illumination one is able to really understand the whole scope of Hindu religion. He was the object-lesson of all the theoretical knowledge given in the Shâstras (scriptures). He showed by his life what the Rishis and Avatâras really wanted to teach. The books were theories, he was the realisation. This man had in fifty-one years lived the five thousand years of national spiritual life and so raised himself to be an object-lesson for future generations. The Vedas can only be explained and the Shastras reconciled by his theory calf Avasthâ or stages — that we must not only tolerate others, but positively embrace them, and that truth is the basis of all religions. Now on these lines a most impressive and beautiful life can be written. Well, everything in good time. Avoid all irregular indecent expressions about sex etc. . ., because other nations think it the height of indecency to mention such things, and his life in English is going to be read by the whole world. I read a Bengali life sent over. It is full of such words. . . .So take care. Carefully avoid such words and expressions. The Calcutta friends have not a cent worth of ability; but they have their assertions of individuality. They are too high to listen to advice. I do not know what to do with these wonderful gentlemen. I have not got much hope in that quarter. *His will be done.* I am simply ashamed of the Bengali book. The writer perhaps thought he was a frank recorder of truth and keeping the very language of Paramahamsa. But he does not remember that Ramakrishna would never use that language before ladies. And this man expects his work to be read by men and women alike! Lord, save me from fools! They, again, have their own freaks; they all knew him! *Bosh and rot.* . . . Beggars taking upon themselves the air of kings! Fools thinking they are all wise! Puny slaves thinking that they are masters! That is their condition. I do not know what to do. Lord save me. I have all hope in Madras. Push on with your work; do not be governed by the Calcutta people. Keep them in good humour in the hope that some one of them may turn good. But push on with your work independently. "Many come to sit at dinner when it is cooked." Take care and work on.

Yours ever with blessings,

VIVEKANANDA.

XXIII

U. S. A.
30th November, 1894.

DEAR KIDI,

. . . As to the wonderful stories published about Shri Ramakrishna, I advise you to keep clear of them and the fools who write them. They are true, but the fools will make a mess of the whole thing, I am sure. He had a whole world of knowledge to teach, why insist upon unnecessary things as miracles really are! They do not prove anything. Matter does not prove Spirit. What connection is there between the existence of God, Soul, or immortality, and the working of miracles? . . . Preach Shri Ramakrishna. Pass the Cup that has satisfied your thirst. . . . Preach Bhakti. Do not disturb your head with metaphysical nonsense, and do not disturb others by your bigotry. . . .

Yours ever with blessings,
VIVEKANANDA.

XXIV

U. S. A.,
26th December, 1894.

BLESSED AND BELOVED, (Alasinga Perumal)

. . . In reference to me every now and then attacks are made in missionary papers (so I hear), but I never care to see them. If you send any of those made in India, I should throw them into the waste-paper basket. A little agitation was necessary for our work. We have had enough. Pay no more attention to what people say about me, whether good or bad. You go on with your work and remember that "Never one meets with evil who tries to do good" (Gita, VI. 40).

Every day the people here are appreciating me. And between you and me, I am more of an influence here than you dream of. Everything must proceed slowly . . . I have written to you before, and I write again, that I shall not pay heed to any criticism or praise in the newspapers. They are consigned to the fire. Do you do the same. Pay no attention whatsoever to newspaper nonsense or criticism. Be sincere and do your duty. Everything will come all right Truth must triumph. . .

Missionary misrepresentations should be beneath sour notice.... Perfect silence is the best refutation to them and I wish you to maintain the same. . . . Make Mr. Subrahmanya Iyer the President of your Society. He is one of the sincerest and noblest men I know; and in him intellect and emotion are beautifully blended. Push on in your work, without counting much on me; work on your own account. . . . As for me, I do not know when I shall go back; I am working here and in India as well. . . .

With my love to you all,

Yours ever with blessings,

VIVEKANANDA.

XXV

541 DEARBORN AVENUE,
Chicago, 1894.

DEAR ALASINGA,

Your letter just to hand. . . . I was mistaken in asking you to publish the scraps I sent you. It was one of my awful mistakes. It shows a moment's weakness. Money can be raised in this country by lecturing for two or three years. But I have tried a little, and although there is much public appreciation of my work, it is thoroughly uncongenial and demoralising to me. . . .

I have read what you say about the Indian papers and their criticisms, which are natural. Jealousy is the central vice of every enslaved race. And it is jealousy and want of combination which cause and perpetuate slavery. You cannot feel the truth of this remark until you come out of India. The secret of Westerners' success is this power of combination, the basis of which is mutual trust and appreciation. The weaker and more cowardly a nation is, so much the more is this sin visible. . . . But, my son, you ought not to expect anything from a slavish race. The case is almost desperate no doubt, but let me put the case before you all. Can you put life into this dead mass — dead to almost all moral aspiration, dead to all future possibilities — and always ready to spring upon those that would try to do good to them? Can you take the position of a physician who tries to pour medicine down the throat of a kicking and refractory child? . . . An American or a European always supports his countrymen in a foreign country. . . . Let me remind you again, "Thou hast the right to work but not to the fruits thereof." Stand firm like a rock. Truth always triumphs. Let the children of Shri Ramakrishna be true to themselves and everything will be all right. We may not live to see the outcome, but as sure as we live, it will come sooner or later. What India wants is a new electric fire to stir up a fresh vigour in the national veins. This was ever, and always will be, slow work. Be content to work, and, above all, be true to yourself. Be pure, staunch, and sincere to the very backbone, and everything will be all right. If you have marked anything in the disciples of Shri Ramakrishna, it is this — they are sincere to the backbone. My task will be done, and I shall be quite content to die, if I can bring up and launch one hundred such men over India. He, the Lord, knows best. Let ignorant men talk nonsense. We neither seek aid nor avoid it — we are the servants of the Most High. The petty attempts of small men should be beneath our notice. Onward! Upon ages of struggle a character is built. Be not discouraged. One word of truth can never be lost; for ages it may be hidden under rubbish, but it will show itself sooner or later. Truth is indestructible, virtue is indestructible, purity is indestructible. Give me a genuine man; I do not want masses of converts. My son, hold fast! Do not care for anybody to help you. Is not the Lord infinitely greater than all human help? Be holy — trust in the Lord, depend on Him always, and you are on the right track; nothing can prevail against you. . . .

Let us pray, "Lead, Kindly Light" — a beam will come through the dark, and a hand will be stretched forth to lead us. I always pray for you: you must pray for me. Let each one of us pray day and night for the downtrodden millions in India who are held fast by poverty, priestcraft, and tyranny — pray day and night for them. I care more to preach religion to them than to the high and the rich. I am no metaphysician, no philosopher, nay, no saint. But I am poor, I love the poor. I see what they call the poor of this country, and how many there are who feel for them! What an immense difference in India! Who feels there for the two hundred millions of men and women sunken for ever in poverty and ignorance? Where is the way out? Who feels for them? They cannot find light or education. Who will bring the light to them — who will travel from door to door bringing education to them? Let these people be your God — think of them, work for them, pray for them incessantly — the Lord will show you the way. Him I call a Mahâtman (great soul) whose heart bleeds for the poor, otherwise he is a Durâtman (wicked soul). Let us unite our wills in continued prayer for their good. We may die unknown, unpitied, unbewailed, without accomplishing anything — but not one thought will be lost. It will take effect, sooner or later. My heart is too full to express my feeling; you know it, you can imagine it. So long as the millions live in hunger and ignorance, I hold every man a traitor who, having been educated at their expense, pays not the least heed to them! I call those men who strut about in their finery, having got all their money by grinding the poor, wretches, so long as they do not do anything for those two hundred millions who are now no better than hungry savages! We are poor, my brothers, we are nobodies, but such have been always the instruments of the Most High. The Lord bless you all.

With all love,

VIVEKANANDA.

XXVI

U. S. A.,
1894.

DEAR DHARMAPALA,

I have forgotten your address in Calcutta; so I direct this to the Math. I heard about your speeches in Calcutta and how wonderful was the effect produced by them. A certain retired missionary here wrote me a letter addressing me as brother and then hastily went to publish my short answer and make a show. But you know what people here think of such gentlemen. Moreover, the same missionary went privately to some of my friends to ask them not to befriend me. Of course he met with universal contempt. I am quite astonished at this man's behaviour — a preacher of religion to take to such underhand dealings! Unfortunately too much of that in every country and in every religion. Last winter I travelled a good deal in this country although the weather was very severe. I thought it would be dreadful, but I did not find it so after all. You remember Col. Neggenson, President of the Free Religious Society. He makes very kind inquiries about you. I met Dr. Carpenter of Oxford (England) the other day. He delivered an address on the ethics of Buddhism at Plymouth. It was very sympathetic and scholarly. He made inquiries about you and your paper. Hope, your noble work will succeed. You are a worthy servant of Him who came Bahujana Hitâya Bahujana Sukhâya (for the good of the many, for the happiness of the many).

. . . The Christianity that is preached in India is quite different from what one sees here; you will be astonished to hear, Dharmapala, that I have friends in this country amongst the clergy of the Episcopal and even Presbyterian churches, who are as broad, as liberal, and as sincere as you are in your own religion. The real spiritual man is broad everywhere. His love forces him to be so. Those to whom religion is a trade are forced to become narrow and mischievous by their introduction into religion of the competitive, fighting, and selfish methods of the world.

Yours ever in brotherly love,

VIVEKANANDA.

XXVII

U. S. A.,
1894.

DEAR ALASINGA,

Listen to an old story. A lazy tramp sauntering along the road saw an old man sitting at the door of his house and stopped to inquire of him the whereabouts of a certain place. "How far is such and such a village?" he asked. The old man remained silent. The man repeated his query several times. Still there was no answer. Disgusted at this, the traveller turned to go away. The old man then stood up and said, "The village of — is only a mile from here." "What!" said the tramp, "Why did you not speak when I asked you before?" "Because then", said the old man, "you seemed so halting and careless about proceeding, but now you are starting off in good earnest, and you have a right to an answer."

Will you remember this story, my son? Go to work, the rest will come: "Whosoever not trusting in anything else but Me, rests on Me, I supply him with everything he needs" (Gitâ, IX. 22). This is no dream.

. . . The work should be in the line of preaching and serving, at the present time. Choose a place of meeting where you can assemble every week holding a service and reading the Upanishads with the commentaries, and so slowly go on learning and working. Everything will come to you if you put your shoulders to the wheel. . .

Now, go to work! G. G.'s nature is of the emotional type, you have a level head; so work together; plunge in; this is only the beginning. Every nation must save itself; we must not depend upon funds from America for the revival of Hinduism, for that is a delusion. To have a centre is a great thing; try to secure such a place in a large town like Madras, end go on radiating a living force in all directions. Begin slowly. Start with a few lay missionaries;

gradually others will come who will devote their whole lives to the work. Do not try to be a ruler. He is the best ruler who can serve well. Be true unto death. The work we want — we do not seek wealth, name or fame. . . . Be brave. . . . Endeavour to interest the people of Madras in collecting funds for the purpose, and then make a beginning. . . . Be perfectly unselfish and you will be sure to succeed. . . . Without losing the independence in work, show all regards to your superiors. Work in harmony. . . . My children must be ready to jump into fire, if needed, to accomplish their work. Now work, work, work! We will stop and compare notes later on. Have patience, perseverance, and purity.

I am writing no book on Hinduism just now. I am simply jotting down my thoughts. I do not know if I shall publish them. What is in books? The world is too full of foolish things already. If you could start a magazine on Vedantic lines, it would further our object. Be positive; do not criticise others. Give your message, teach what you have to teach, and there stop. The Lord knows the rest. . . .

Do not send me any more newspapers, as I do not notice the missionary criticisms on myself; and here the public estimation of me is better for that reason.

. . . If you are really my children, you will fear nothing, stop at nothing. You will be like lions. We must rouse India and the whole world. No cowardice. I will take no nay. Do you understand? Be true unto death! . . . The secret of this is Guru-Bhakti — faith in the Guru unto death! Have you that? I believe with all my heart that you have, and you know that I have confidence in you — so go to work. You must succeed. My prayers and benedictions follow every step you take. Work in harmony. Be patient with everybody. Every one has my love. I am watching you. Onward! Onward! This is just the beginning. My little work here makes a big echo in India, do you know? So I shall not return there in a hurry. My intention is to do something permanent here, and with that object I am working day by day. I am every day gaining the confidence of the American people. . . . Expand your hearts and hopes, as wide as the world. Study Sanskrit, especially the three Bhâshyas (commentaries) on the Vedanta. Be ready, for I have many plans for the future. Try to be a magnetic speaker. Electrify the people. Everything will come to you if you have faith. So tell Kidi, in fact, tell all my children there. In time they will do great things at which the world will wonder. Take heart and work. Show me something you have done. Show me a temple, a press, a paper, a home for me. Where shall I come to if you cannot make a home for me in Madras? Electrify people. Raise funds and preach. Be true to your mission. Thus far you promise well, so go on and do better and better still.

. . .Do not fight with people; do not antagonise anyone. Why should we mind if Jack and John become Christians? Let them follow whatever religion suits them. Why should you mix in controversies? Bear with the various opinions of everybody. Patience, purity, and perseverance will prevail.

Yours etc.,

VIVEKANANDA.

XXVIII

541 DEARBORN AVENUE,
CHICAGO,
3rd January, 1895.

DEAR MRS. BULL,

I lectured at Brooklyn last Sunday, Mrs. Higgins gave a little reception the evening I arrived, and some of the prominent members of the Ethical Society including Dr. Jain [Janes] were there. Some of them thought that such Oriental religious subjects will not interest the Brooklyn public.

But the lecture, through the blessings of the Lord, proved a tremendous success. About 800 of the *élite* of Brooklyn were present, and the very gentlemen who thought it would not prove a success are trying for organising a series in Brooklyn. The New York course for me is nearly ready, but I do not wish to fix the dates until Miss Thursby comes to New York. As such Miss Phillips who is a friend of Miss Thursby's and who is arranging the New York course for me will act with Miss Thursby in case she wants to get up something in New York.

I owe much to the Hale family and I thought to give them a little surprise by dropping in on New Year's day. I am trying to get a new gown here. The old gown is here, but it is so shrunken by constant washings that it is unfit to wear in public. I am almost confident of finding the exact thing in Chicago.

I hope your father is all right by this time.

With my love to Miss Farmer, Mr. and Mrs. Gibbons and the rest of the holy family, I am ever yours,

Affectionately,

VIVEKANANDA.

PS. I saw Miss Couring at Brooklyn. She was as kind as ever. Give her my love if you write her soon.

XXIX

CHICAGO,
11th January, 1895.

DEAR G. G, (G. G. Narasimhachariar)

Your letter just to hand. . . . The Parliament of Religions was organised with the intention of proving the superiority of the Christian religion over other forms of faith, but the philosophic religion of Hinduism was able to maintain its position notwithstanding. Dr. Barrows and the men of that ilk are very orthodox, and I do not look to them for help. . . . The Lord has sent me many friends in this country, and they are always on the increase. The Lord bless those who have tried to injure me. . . . I have been running all the time between Boston and New York, two great centres of this country, of which Boston may be called the brain and New York, the purse. In both, my success is more than ordinary. I am indifferent to the newspaper reports, and you must not expect me to send any of them to you. A little boom was necessary to begin work. We have had more than enough of that.

I have written to Mani Iyer, and I have given you my directions already. *Now show me what you can do.* No foolish talk now, but actual work; the Hindus must back their talk with real work; if they cannot they do not deserve anything; that is all. America is not going to give you money for your fads. And why should they? As for me, I want to teach the truth; I do not care whether here or elsewhere.

In future do not pay any heed to what people say either for or against you or me. Work on, be lions; and the Lord will bless you. I shall work incessantly until I die, and even after death I shall work for the good of the world. Truth is infinitely more weighty than untruth; so is goodness. If you possess these, they will make their way by sheer gravity.

I have no connection with the Theosophists. And Judge will help me — pooh! . . . Thousands of the best men *do* care for me; you know this, and have faith in the Lord. I am slowly exercising an influence in this land greater than all the newspaper blazoning of me can do. The orthodox feel it, but they cannot help it. It is the force of character, of purity, and of truth — of personality. So long as I have these things, you can feel easy; no one will be able to injure a hair of my head. If they try, they will fail, saith the Lord. . . . Enough of books and theories. It is the *life* that is the highest and the only way to stir the hearts of people; it carries the personal magnetism. . . . The Lord is giving me a deeper and deeper insight every day. Work, work, work. . . . Truce to foolish talk; talk of the Lord. Life is too short to be spent in talking about frauds and cranks

You must always remember that every nation must save itself; so must every man; do not look to others for help. Through hard work here, I shall be able now and then to send you a little money for your work; but that is all. If you have to look forward to that, better stop work. Know also that this is a grand field for my ideas, and that I do not care whether they are Hindus or Mohammedans or Christians, but those that love the Lord will always command my service.

. . . I like to work on calmly and silently, and the Lord is always with me. Follow me, if you will, by being intensely sincere, perfectly unselfish, and, above all, by being perfectly pure. My blessings go with you. In this short life there is no time for the exchange of compliments. We can compare notes and compliment each other to our hearts' content after the battle is finished. Now, do not talk; work, work! work! I do not see anything permanent you have done in India — I do not see any centre you have made — I do not see any temple or hall you have erected — I do not see anybody joining hands with you. There is too much talk, talk, talk! We are great, we are great! Nonsense! We are imbeciles; that is what we are! This hankering after name and fame and all other humbugs — what are they to me? What do I care about them? I should like to see hundreds coming to the Lord! Where are they? I want them, I want to see them. You must seek them out. You only give me name and fame. Have done with name and fame; to work, my brave men, to work! You have not caught my fire yet — you do not understand me! You run in the old ruts of sloth and enjoyments. Down with all sloth, down with all enjoyments here or hereafter. Plunge into the fire and bring the people towards the Lord.

That you may catch my fire, that you may be intensely sincere, that you may die the heroes' death on the field of battle — is the constant prayer of

VIVEKANANDA.

PS. Tell Alasinga, Kidi, Dr. Balaji, and all the others not to pin their faith on what Tom, Dick, and Harry say for or against us, but to concentrate all their energy on work.

XXX

U.S.A.,
12th January, 1895.

DEAR ALASINGA,

I am sorry you still continue to send me pamphlets and newspapers, which I have written you several times not to do. I have no time to peruse them and take notice of them. Please send them *no more*. I do not care a fig for what the missionaries or the Theosophists say about me. Let them do as they please. The very taking notice of them will be to give them importance. Besides, you know, the missionaries only abuse and never argue.

Now know once and for all that I do not care for name or fame, or any humbug of that type. I want to preach my ideas for the good of the world. You have done a great work; but so far as it goes, it has only given me name and fame. My life is more precious than spending it in getting the admiration of the world. I have no time for such foolery. What work have you done in the way of advancing the ideas and organising in India? *None, none, none*!

An organisation that will teach the Hindus mutual help and appreciation is absolutely necessary. Five thousand people attended that meeting that was held in Calcutta, and hundreds did the same in other places, to express an appreciation of my work here — well and good! But if you asked them each to give an anna, would they do it? The whole national character is one of childish dependence. They are all ready to enjoy food if it is brought to their mouth, and even some want it pushed down. . . . You do not deserve to live if you cannot help yourselves.

I have given up at present my plan for the education of the masses. It will come by degrees. What I now want is a band of fiery missionaries. We must have a *College* in Madras to teach comparative religions, Sanskrit, the different schools of Vedanta, and some European languages; we must have a press, and papers printed in English and in the Vernaculars. When this is done, then I shall know that you have accomplished something. Let the nation show that they are ready to *do*. If you cannot do anything of the kind in India, then let me alone. I have a message to give, let me give it to the people who appreciate it and who will work it out. What care I who takes it? "He who doeth the will of my Father," is my own. . . .

My name should not be made prominent; it is my ideas that I want to see realised. The disciples of all the prophets have always inextricably mixed up the ideas of the Master with the *person,* and at last killed the ideas for the *person*. The disciples of Shri Ramakrishna must guard against doing the same thing. Work for the *idea,* not the person. The Lord bless you.

Yours ever with blessings,

VIVEKANANDA.

XXXI

BROOKLYN,
20th January, 1895.

(Written to Mrs. Ole Bull whom Swamiji called "Dhirâ Mâtâ", the "Steady Mother" on the occasion of the loss of her father.)

. . . I had a premonition of your father's giving up the old body and it is not my custom to write to anyone when a wave of would-be inharmonious Mâyâ strikes him. But these are the great turning points in life, and I know that you are unmoved. The surface of the sea rises and sinks alternately, but to the observant soul — the child of light — each sinking reveals more and more of the depth and of the beds of pearls and coral at the bottom. Coming and going is all pure delusion. The soul never comes nor goes. Where is the place to which it shall go when all space is *in the soul*? When shall be the time for entering and departing when all time is *in the soul*?

The earth moves, causing the illusion of the movement of the sun; but the sun does not move. So Prakriti, or Maya, or Nature, is moving, changing, unfolding veil after veil, turning over leaf after leaf of this grand book — while the witnessing soul drinks in knowledge, unmoved, unchanged. All souls that ever have been, are, or shall be, are all in the present tense and — to use a material simile — are all standing at one geometrical point. Because the idea of space does occur in the soul, therefore all that were ours, are ours, and will *be* ours, *are* always with us, *were* always with us, and *will* be always with us. We are in them. They are in us. Take these cells. Though each separate, they are all nevertheless inseparably joined at A B. There they are one.

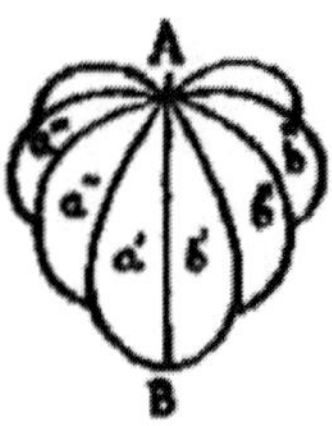

Each is an individual, yet all are one at the axis A B. None can escape from that axis, and however broken or torn the circumference, yet by standing at the axis, we may enter any one of the chambers. This axis is the Lord. There we are one with Him, all in all, and all in God.

The cloud moves across the face of the moon, creating the illusion that the moon is moving. So nature, body, matter moves on, creating the illusion that the soul is moving. Thus we find at last that, that instinct (or inspiration?) which men of every race, whether high or low, have had to feel, viz the presence of the departed about them, is true intellectually also.

Each soul is a star, and all stars are set in that infinite azure, that eternal sky, the Lord. There is the root, the reality, the real individuality of each and all. Religion began with the search after some of these stars that had passed beyond our horizon, and ended in finding them all in God, and ourselves in the same place. The whole secret is, then, that your father has given up the old garment he was wearing and is standing where he was through all eternity. Will he manifest another such garment in this or any other world? I sincerely pray that he may not, until he does so in full consciousness. I pray that none may be dragged anywhither by the unseen power of his own past actions. I pray that all may be free, that is to say, may know that they are free. And if they are to dream again, let us pray that their dreams be all of peace and bliss. . . .

Yours etc.,

VIVEKANANDA.

XXXII

54 W. 33RD STREET, N.Y.,
1st February, 1895.

DEAR SISTER (Miss Mary Hale)

I just received your beautiful note.... Well, sometimes it is a good discipline to be forced to work for work's sake, even to the length of not being allowed to enjoy the fruits of one's labour.... I am very glad of your criticisms and am not sorry at all. The other day at Miss Thursby's I had an excited argument with a Presbyterian gentleman, who, as usual, got very hot, angry, and abusive. However, I was afterwards severely reprimanded by Mrs. Bull for this, as such things hinder my work. So, it seems, is your opinion.

I am glad you write about it just now, because I have been giving a good deal of thought to it. In the first place, I am not at all sorry for these things — perhaps that may disgust you — it may. I know full well how good it is for one's worldly prospects to be *sweet*. I do everything to be *sweet*, but when it comes to a horrible compromise with the truth within, then I stop. I do not believe in humility. I believe in *Samadarshitva* — same state of mind with regard to all. The duty of the ordinary man is to obey the commands of his "God", society; but the children of light never do so. This is an eternal law. One accommodates himself to surroundings and social opinion and gets all good things from society, the giver of all good to such. The other stands alone and draws society up towards him. The accommodating man finds a path of roses; the non-accommodating, one of thorns. But the worshippers of "Vox populi" go to annihilation in a moment; the children of truth *live for ever*.

I will compare truth to a corrosive substance of infinite power. It burns its way in wherever it falls — in soft substance at once, hard granite slowly, but it must. What is writ is writ. I am so, so sorry, Sister, that I cannot make myself sweet and accommodating to every black falsehood. But I cannot. I have suffered for it all my life. But I cannot. I have essayed and essayed. But I cannot. At last I have given it up. The Lord is great. He will not allow me to become a hypocrite. Now let what is in come out. I have not found a way that will please all, and I cannot but be what I am, true to my own self. "Youth and beauty vanish, life and wealth vanish, name and fame vanish, even the mountains crumble into dust. Friendship and love vanish. Truth alone abides." God of Truth, be Thou alone my guide! I am too old to change now into milk and honey. Allow me to remain as I am. "Without fear — without shopkeeping, caring neither for friend nor foe, do thou hold on to Truth, Sannyâsin, and from this moment give up this world and the next and all that are to come — their enjoyments and their vanities. Truth, be thou alone my guide." I have no desire for wealth or name or fame or enjoyments, Sister — they are dust unto me. I wanted to help my brethren. I have not the *tact to earn money,* bless the Lord. What reason is there for me to conform to the vagaries of the world around me and not obey the voice of Truth within? The mind is still weak, Sister, it sometimes mechanically clutches at earthly help. But I am not afraid. Fear is the greatest sin my religion teaches.

The last fight with the Presbyterian priest and the long fight afterwards with Mrs. Bull showed me in a clear light what Manu says to the Sannyasin, "Live alone, walk alone." All friendship, all love, is only limitation. There never was a friendship, especially of women, which was not exacting. O great sages! You were right. One cannot serve the God of Truth who leans upon somebody. Be still, my soul! Be alone! and the Lord is with you. Life is nothing! Death is a delusion! All this is not, God alone is! Fear not, my soul! Be alone. Sister, the way is long, the time is short, evening is approaching. I have to go home soon. I have no time to give my manners a finish. I cannot find time to deliver my message. You are good, you are so kind, I will do anything for you; and do not be angry, I see you all are mere children.

Dream no more! Oh, dream no more, my soul! In one word, I have a message to give, I have no time to be sweet to the world, and every attempt at sweetness makes me a hypocrite. I will die a thousand deaths rather than lead a jelly-fish existence and yield to every requirement of this foolish world, no matter whether it be my own country or a foreign country. You are mistaken, utterly mistaken, if you think I have a *work,* as Mrs. Bull thinks; I have no *work* under or beyond the sun. I have a message, and I will give it after my own fashion. I will neither Hinduise my message, nor Christianise it, nor make it any "ise" in the world. I will only my-ise it and that is all. *Liberty,* Mukti, is all my religion, and everything that tries to curb it, I will avoid by fight or flight. Pooh! I try to pacify the priests!! Sister, do not take this amiss. But you are babies and babies must submit to be taught. You have not yet drunk of that fountain which makes "reason unreason, mortal immortal, this world a zero, and of man a God". Come out if you can of this network of foolishness they call this *world*. Then I will call you indeed brave and free. If you cannot, cheer those that dare dash this false God, society, to the ground and trample on its unmitigated hypocrisy; if you cannot cheer them, pray, be silent, but do not try to drag them down again into the mire with such false nonsense as *compromise* and becoming nice and sweet.

I hate this world, this dream, this horrible nightmare with its churches and chicaneries, its books and blackguardisms, its fair faces and false hearts, its howling righteousness on the surface and utter hollowness beneath, and, above all, its sanctified shopkeeping. What! measure any soul according to what the bond-slaves of the world say? — Pooh! Sister, you do not know the Sannyasin. "He stands on the heads of the Vedas!" say the Vedas, because he is free from churches and sects and religions and prophets and books and all of that ilk! Missionary or no missionary, let them howl and attack me with all they can, I take them as Bhartrihari says, "Go thou thy ways, Sannyasin! Some will say, 'Who is this mad man?' Others, 'Who is this Chandâla?' Others will know thee to be a sage. Be glad at the prattle of the worldlings." But when they attack, know that, "The elephant passing through the market-place is always beset by curs, but he cares not. He goes straight on *his own way*. So it is always, when a great soul appears there will be numbers to bark after him." (Tulasidasa)

I am living with Landsberg at 54 W. 33rd Street. He is a brave and noble soul, Lord bless him. Sometimes I go to the Guernseys' to sleep.

Lord bless you all ever and ever — and may He lead you quickly out of this big humbug, the world! May you never be enchanted by this old witch, the world! May Shankara help you! May Umâ open the door of truth for you and take away all your delusions!

Yours with love and blessings,

VIVEKANANDA.

XXXIII

19 W., 38 ST.,
NEW YORK, 1895.

DEAR ALASINGA,

. . . Meddle not with so-called social reform, for there cannot be any reform without spiritual reform first. Who told you that I want social reform? Not I. Preach the Lord — say neither good nor bad about the superstitions and diets. Do not lose heart, do not lose faith in your Guru, do not lose faith in God. So long as you possess these three, nothing can harm you, my child. I am growing stronger every day. Work on, my brave boys.

Ever yours with blessings,

VIVEKANANDA.

XXXIV

54 WEST, 33 NEW YORK,
25th February, 1895.

DEAR SISTER,

I am sorry you had an attack of illness. I will give you an absent treatment though your confession takes half the strength out of my mind.

That you have rolled put of it is all right. All's well that ends well.

The books have arrived in good condition and many thanks for them.

Your ever affectionate bro.,

VIVEKANANDA.

XXXV

U. S. A.,
6th March, 1895.

DEAR ALASINGA,

. . . Do not for a moment think the "Yankees" are practical in religion. In that the Hindu alone is practical, the Yankee in money-making, so that as soon as I depart, the whole thing will disappear. Therefore I want to have a solid ground under my feet before I depart. Every work should be made thorough. . . . You need not insist upon preaching Shri Ramakrishna. Propagate his ideas first, though I know the world always wants the Man first, then the idea. . . . Do not figure out big plans at first, but begin slowly, feel your ground, and proceed up and up.

. . . Work on, my brave boys. We shall see the light some day.

Harmony and peace! . . . Let things slowly grow. Rome was not built in a day. The Maharaja of Mysore is dead — one of our greatest hopes. Well! the Lord is great. He will send others to help the cause.

Send some Kushâsanas (small sitting-mats) if you can.

Yours ever with blessings,

VIVEKANANDA.

XXXVI

54 W., 33 NEW YORK,
27th March, 1895.

DEAR SISTER (Isabelle McKindley)

Your kind note gave me pleasure inexpressible. I was also able to read it through very easily. I have at last hit upon the orange and have got a coat, but could not as yet get any in summer material. If you get any, kindly inform me. I will have it made here in New York. Your wonderful Dearborn Ave. misfit tailor is too much even for a *monk*.

Sister Locke writes me a long letter and perhaps wondering at my delay in reply. She is apt to be carried away by enthusiasm; so I am waiting, and again I do not know what to answer. Kindly tell her from me that it is impossible for me to fix any place just now. Mrs. Peake though noble, grand, and very spiritual, is as much clever in worldly matter as I, yet I am getting cleverer every day. Mrs. Peake has been offered, by some one whom she knows only hazily in Washington, a place for summer.

Who knows that she will not be played upon? This is a wonderful country for cheating, and 99.9 per cent have some *motive* in the background to take advantage of others. If any one just but closes his eyes for a moment, he is *gone*!! Sister Josephine is fiery. Mrs. Peake is a simple good woman. I have been so well handled by the people here that I look round me for hours before I take a step. Everything will come to right. Ask Sister Josephine to have a little patience.

You are every day finding kindergarten better than running an old man's home I am sure. You saw Mrs. Bull, and I am sure you were quite surprised to find her so tame and gentle. Do you see Mrs. Adams now and then? Mrs. Bull has been greatly benefited by her lessons. I also took a few, but no use; the ever increasing load in front does not allow me to bend forward as Mrs. Adams wants it. If I try to bend forward in walking, the centre of gravity comes to the surface of the stomach, and so I go cutting front somersaults.

No millionaire coming? Not even a few hundred thousands? Sorry, very sorry!!! I am trying my best; what I can do? My classes are full of women. You of course cannot marry a woman. Well, have patience. I will keep my eyes open and never let go an opportunity. If you do not get one, it would not be owing to any laziness at least on my part.

Life goes on the same old ruts. Sometimes I get disgusted with eternal lecturings and talkings, want to be silent for days and days.

Hoping you the best dreams (for that is the only way to be happy).

I remain ever your loving bro.,

VIVEKANANDA.

XXXVII

U. S. A.,
4th April, 1895.

DEAR ALASINGA,

Your letter just to hand. You need not be afraid of anybody's attempting to hurt me. So long as the Lord protects me I shall be impregnable. Your ideas of America are very hazy. . . . This is a huge country, the majority do not care much about religion. . . . Christianity holds its ground as a mere patriotism, and nothing more.

. . . Now my son, do not lose courage. . . . Send me the *Vedanta-Sutras* and the Bhâshyas (commentaries) of all the sects.... I am in His hands. What is the use of going back to India? India cannot further my ideas. This country takes kindly to my ideas. I will go back when I get the Command. In the meanwhile, do you all gently and patiently work. If anybody attacks me, simply ignore his existence. . . . My idea is for you to start a Society where people could be taught the Vedas and the Vedanta, with the commentaries. Work on this line at present. . . . Know that every time you feel weak, you not only hurt yourself but also the Cause. Infinite faith and strength are the only conditions of success.

Be cheerful. . . . Hold on to your own ideal. . . . Above all, never attempt to guide or rule others, or, as the Yankees say, "boss" others. Be the servant of all.

Ever yours with blessings,
VIVEKANANDA.

XXXVIII

U. S. A.,
2nd May, 1895.

DEAR S— ,

So you have made up your mind to renounce the world. I have sympathy with your desire. There is nothing so high as renunciation of self. But you must not forget that to forgo your own favourite desire for the welfare of those that depend upon you is no small sacrifice. Follow the spotless life and teachings of Shri Ramakrishna and look after the comforts of your family. You do your own duty, and leave the rest to Him.

Love makes no distinction between man and man, between an Aryan and a Mlechchha, between a Brâhmana and a Pariah, nor even between a man and a woman. Love makes the whole universe as one's own home. True progress is slow but sure. Work among those young men who can devote heart and soul to this one duty — the duty of raising the masses of India. Awake them, unite them, and inspire them with this spirit of renunciation; it depends wholly on the young people of India.

Cultivate the virtue of obedience, but you must not sacrifice your own faith. No centralization is possible unless there is obedience to superiors. No great work can be done without this centralization of individual forces. The Calcutta Math is the main centre; the members of all other branches must act in unity and conformity with the rules of that centre.

Give up jealousy and conceit. Learn to work unitedly for others. This is the great need of our country.

Yours with blessings,

VIVEKANANDA.

XXXIX

U. S. A.,
6th May, 1895.

DEAR ALASINGA,

This morning I received your last letter and that first volume of the Bhâshya of Râmânujâcharya. A few days ago I received another letter from you. Also I received a letter from Mr. Mani Iyer. I am doing well and going on in the same old rate. You mention about the lectures of Mr. Lund. I do not know who he is or where he is. He may be some one lecturing in Churches; for had he big platforms, we would have heard of him. Maybe, he gets them reported in some newspapers and sends them to India; and the missionaries may be making trade out of it. Well, so far I guess from the tone of your letters. It is no public affair here to call forth any defence from us; for in that case I will have to fight hundreds of them here every day. For India is now in the air, and the orthodox, including Dr. Barrows and all the rest, are struggling hard to put out the fire. In the second place, every one of these orthodox lectures against India must have a good deal of abuse hurled against me. If you hear some of the filthy stories the orthodox men and women invent against me, you will be astonished. Now, do you mean to say that a Sannyâsin should go about defending himself against the brutal and cowardly attacks of these self-seeking men and women? I have some very influential friends here who, now and then, give them their quietus. Again, why should I waste my energies defending Hinduism if the Hindus all go to sleep? What are you three hundred millions of people doing there, especially those that are so proud of their learning etc.? Why do you not take up the fighting and leave me to teach and preach? Here am I struggling day and night in the midst of strangers.... What help does India send? Did the world ever see a nation with less patriotism than the Indian? If you could send and maintain for a few years a dozen well-educated strong men to preach in Europe and America, you would do immense service to India, both morally and politically. Every man who morally sympathises with India becomes a political friend. Many of the Western people think of you as a nation of half-naked savages, and therefore only fit to be whipped into civilization. If you three hundred millions become cowed by the missionaries — you cowards — and dare not say a word, what can one man do in a far distant land? Even what I have done, you do not deserve.

Why do you not send your defences to the American magazines? What prevents you? You race of cowards — physical, moral, and spiritual! You animals fit to be treated as you are with two ideas before you — lust and money — you want to prod a Sannyasin to a life of constant fighting, and you are afraid of the "Saheb logs", even missionaries! And you will do great things, pish! Why not some of you write a beautiful defence and send it to the Arena Publishing Company of Boston? The *Arena* is a magazine which will gladly publish it and perhaps pay you hard money. So far it ends. Think of this when you will be tempted to be a fool. Think that up to date every blackguard of a Hindu that had hitherto come to western lands had too often criticised his own faith and country in order to get praise or money. You know that I did not come to seek name and fame; it was forced upon me. Why shall I go back to India? Who will help me? . . . You are children, you prattle you do not know what. Where are the men in Madras who will give up the world to preach religion? Worldliness and realization of God cannot go together. I am the one man who dared defend his country, and I have given them such ideas as they never expected from a Hindu. There are many who are against me, but I will never be a coward like you. There are also thousands in the country who are my friends, and hundreds who would follow me unto death; every year they will increase, and if I live and work with them, my ideals of life and religion will be fulfilled. Do you see?

I do not hear much now about the Temple Universal that was to be built in America; yet I have a firm footing in New York, the very centre of American life, and so my work will go on. I am taking several of my disciples to a summer retreat to finish their training in Yoga and Bhakti and Jnâna, and then they will be able to help carry the work on. Now my boys, go to work.

Within a month I shall be in a position to send some money for the paper. Do not go about begging from the Hindu beggars. I will do it all *myself* with my own brain and strong right hand. I do not want the help of any man here or in India. . . . Do not press too much the Ramakrishna Avatâra.

Now I will tell you my discovery. All of religion is contained in the Vedanta, that is, in the three stages of the Vedanta philosophy, the Dvaita, Vishishtâdvaita and Advaita; one comes after the other. These are the three stages of spiritual growth in man. Each one is necessary. This is the essential of religion: the Vedanta, applied to the various ethnic customs and creeds of India, is Hinduism. The first stage, i.e. Dvaita, applied to the ideas of the ethnic groups of Europe, is Christianity; as applied to the Semitic groups, Mohammedanism. The Advaita, as applied in its Yoga-perception form, is Buddhism etc. Now by religion is meant the Vedanta; the applications must vary according to the different needs, surroundings, and other circumstances of different nations. You will find that although the philosophy is the same, the Shâktas, Shaivas, etc. apply it each to their own special cult and *forms*. Now, in your journal write article after article on these three systems, showing their harmony as one following after the other, and at the same time keeping off the ceremonial forms altogether. That is, preach the philosophy, the spiritual part, and let people suit it to their own forms. I wish to write a book on this subject, therefore I wanted the three Bhashyas; but only one volume of the Ramanuja (Bhashya) has reached me as yet.

The American Theosophists have seceded from the others, and now they hate India. Poor things! And Sturdy of England who has lately been in India and met my brother Shivananda wrote me a letter wanting to know when I go over to England. I wrote him a nice letter. What about Babu Akshay Kumar Ghosh? I do not hear anything from him more. Give the missionaries and others their dues. Get up some of our very strong men and write a nice, strong, but good-toned article on the present religious revival in India and send it to some American magazine. I am acquainted with only one or two of them. You know I am not much of a writer. I am not in the habit of going from door to door begging. I sit quiet and let things come to me. . . . Now, my children, I could have made a grand success in the way of organising here, if I were a worldly hypocrite. Alas! That is all of religion here; money and name = priest, money and lust = layman. I am to create a new order of humanity here who are sincere believers in God and care nothing for the world. This must be slow, very slow. In the meantime you go on with your work, and I shall steer my boat straight ahead. The journal must not be flippant but steady, calm, and high-toned. . . . Get hold of a band of fine, steady writers. . . . Be perfectly unselfish, be steady and work on. We will do great things; do not fear. . . . One thing more. Be the servant of all, and do not try in the least to govern others. That will excite jealousy and destroy everything. . . . Go on. You have worked wonderfully well. We do not wait for help, we will work it out, my boy, be self-reliant, faithful and patient. Do not antagonise my other friends, live in harmony with all. My eternal love to all.

Ever yours with blessings,

VIVEKANANDA.

PS. Nobody will come to help you if you put yourself forward as a leader. . . . Kill self first if you want to succeed.

XL

NEW YORK,
14th May, 1895.

DEAR ALASINGA,

. . . Now I have got a hold on New York, and I hope to get a permanent body of workers who will carry on the work when I leave the country. Do you see, my boy, all this newspaper blazoning is nothing? I ought to be able to leave a permanent effect behind me when I go; and with the blessings of the Lord it is going to be very soon. . . . *Men* are more valuable than all the wealth of the world.

You need not worry about me. The Lord is always protecting me. My coming to this country and all my labours must not be in vain.

The Lord is merciful, and although there are many who try to injure me any way they can, there are many also who will befriend me to the last. Infinite patience, infinite purity, and infinite perseverance are the secret of success in a good cause.

Ever yours with blessings,
VIVEKANANDA.

XLI

C/O MISS DUTCHER,
THOUSAND ISLAND PARK, N.Y.,
18th June, 1895.

DEAR FRIEND, (Mr. F. Leggett)

A letter reached me from Mrs. Sturges the day before she left, including a cheque for $50. It was impossible to make the acknowledgement reach her the next day; so I take this opportunity to ask you the favour of sending her my thanks and acknowledgement in your next to her.

We are having a nice time here except, as an old Hindu proverb says, that "a pestle must pound even if it goes to heaven". I have to work hard all the same. I am going to Chicago in the beginning of August. When are you starting?

All our friends here send their respects to you. Hoping you all bliss and joy and health, and ever praying for the same.

I remain, yours affectionately,

VIVEKANANDA.

XLII

19 W 38TH ST., NEW YORK
22nd June, 1895

DEAR KIDI,

I will write you a whole letter instead of a line. I am glad you are progressing. You are mistaken in thinking that I am not going to return to India; I am coming soon. I am not giving to failures, and here I have planted a seed, and it is going to become a tree, and it must. Only I am afraid it will hurt its growth if I give it up too soon. . . .

Work on, my boy. Rome was not built in a day. I am guided by the Lord, so everything will come all right in the end.

With my love ever and ever to you,

Yours sincerely,

VIVEKANANDA.

XLIII

U. S. A.,
1st July, 1895.

DEAR ALASINGA,

I received your missionary book and the Ramnad photos. I have written to the Raja as well as the Dewan at Mysore. The missionary pamphlet must have reached here long ago, as the Ramabai circle controversy with Dr. Janes savoured of it, it seems. Now you need not be afraid of anything. There is one misstatement in that pamphlet. I never went to a big hotel in this country, and very few times to any other. At Baltimore, the small hotels, being ignorant, would not take in a black man, thinking him a negro. So my host, Dr. Vrooman, had to take me to a larger one, because they knew the difference between a negro and a foreigner. Let me tell you, Alasinga, that you have to defend yourselves. Why do you behave like babies? If anybody attacks your religion, why cannot, you defend it? As for me, you need not be afraid, I have more friends than enemies here, and in this country one-third are Christians, and only a small number of the educated care about the missionaries. Again, the very fact of the missionaries being against anything makes the educated like it. They are less of a power here now, and are becoming less so every day. If their attacks pain you, why do you behave like a petulant child and refer to me? . . . Cowardice is no virtue.

Here I have already got a respectable following. Next year I will organise it on a working basis, and then the work will be carried on. And when I am off to India, I have friends who will back me here and help me in India too; so you need not fear. So long as you shriek at the missionary attempts and jump without being able to do anything, I laugh at you; you are little dollies, that is what you are. . . . What can Swami do for old babies!!

I know, my son, I shall have to come and manufacture men out of you. I know that India is only inhabited by women and eunuchs. So do not fret. I will have to get means to work there. I do not put myself in the hands of imbeciles. You need not worry, do what little you can. I have to work alone from top to bottom. . . . "This Âtman (Self) is not to be reached by cowards."

You need not be afraid for me. The Lord is with me, you defend yourselves only and show me you can do that; and I will be satisfied. Don't bother me any more with what any one says about me. I am not waiting to hear any fool's judgment of me. You babies, great results are attained only by great patience, great courage, and great attempts. . . . Kidi's mind is taking periodic somersaults, I am afraid. . . .

The brave alone do great things, not the cowards. Know once for all, you faithless ones, that I am in the hands of the Lord. So long as I am pure and His servant, not a hair of my head will be touched. . . . Do something for the nation, then they will help you, then the nation will be with you. Be brave, be brave! Man dies but once. My disciples must not be cowards.

Ever yours with love,

VIVEKANANDA.

XLIV

THOUSAND ISLAND PARK,
29th (July?), 1895.

A glorious time to you, dear Mother (Mrs. William Sturges.) and I am sure this letter will find you in all health. Many thanks for the $50 you sent; it went a long way.

We have had such a nice time here. Two ladies came up all the way from Detroit to be with us here. They are so pure and good. I am going from the Thousand Island to Detroit and thence to Chicago.

Our class in New York is going on, and they have carried it bravely on, although I was not there.

By the by, the two ladies who have come from Detroit were in the class, and unfortunately were mighty frightened with imps and other persons of that ilk. They have been taught to put a little salt, just a little, in burning alcohol, and if there is a black precipitate, that must be the impurities showing the presence of the imps. However, these two ladies had too much fright from the imps. It is said that these imps are everywhere filling the whole universe. Father Leggett must be awfully downcast at your absence, as I did not hear from him up to date. Well, it is better to let grief have its way. So I do not bother him any more.

Aunt Joe Joe must have had a terrible time at sea. All is well that ends well.

The babies (Hollister and Alberta — then at school in Germany) must be enjoying their stay in Germany very much. My shiploads of love to them.

We all here send you love, and I wish you a life that will be like a torch to generations to come.

Your son,

VIVEKANANDA.

XLV

C/O MISS DUTCHER,
THOUSAND ISLAND PARK,
July, 1895.

DEAR MOTHER, (Mrs. Betty Sturges.)

I am sure you are in New York by this time, and that it is not very hot there now.

We are having great times here. Marie Louise arrived yesterday. So we are exactly seven now including all that have come yet.

All the sleep of the world has come upon me. I sleep at least two hours during the day and sleep through the whole night as a piece of log. This is a reaction, I think, from the sleeplessness of New York. I am also writing and reading a little, and have a class every morning after breakfast. The meals are being conducted on the strictest vegetarian principles, and I am fasting a good deal.

I am determined that several pounds of my fat shall be off before I leave. This is a Methodist place, and they will have their camp meeting in August. It is a very beautiful spot, but I am afraid it becomes too crowded during the season.

Miss Joe Joe's fly-bite has been cured completely by this time, I am sure Where is . . . Mother? Kindly give her my best regards when you write her next.

I will always look back upon the delightful time I had at Percy, and always thank Mr. Leggett for that treat I shall be able to go to Europe with him. When you meet him next, kindly give him my eternal love and gratitude. The world is always bettered by the love of the likes of him.

Are you with your friend, Mrs. Dora (long German name). She is a noble soul, a genuine Mahâtmâ (great soul). Kindly give her my love and regards.

I am in a sort of sleepy, lazy, happy state now and do not seem to dislike it. Marie Louise brought a little tortoise from New York, her pet. Now, arriving here, the pet found himself surrounded with his natural element. So by dint of persistent tumbling and crawling, he has left the love and fondlings of Marie Louise far, far behind. She was a little sorry at first, but we preached liberty with such a vigour that she had to come round quick

May the Lord bless you and yours for ever and ever is the constant prayer of

VIVEKANANDA

PS. Joe Joe did not send the birch bark book. Mrs. Bull was very glad to have the one I had sent her.

I had a large number of very beautiful letters from India Everything is all right there. Send my love to the babies on the other side — the real "innocents abroad".

V.

XLVI

C/O MISS DUTCHER,
THOUSAND ISLAND PARK, N. Y.
7th July, 1895.

DEAR FRIEND, (Mr. F. Leggett)

I see you are enjoying New York very much, so excuse my breaking into your reverie with a letter.

I had two beautiful letters from Miss MacLeod and Mrs. Sturges. Also they sent over two pretty birch bark books. I have filled them with Sanskrit texts and translations, and they go by today's post.

Mrs. Dora is giving, I hear, some startling performances in the Mahatma line.

Since leaving Percy I have invitations to come over to London from unexpected quarters, and that I look forward to with great expectations.

I do not want to lose this opportunity of working in London. And so your invitation, coupled with the London one, is, I know, a divine call for further work.

I shall be here all this month and only have to go to Chicago for a few days sometime in August.

Don't fret, Father Leggett, this is the best time for expectation — when sure in love.

Lord bless you ever and ever, and may all happiness be yours for ever, as you richly deserve it.

Ever yours in love and affection,

VIVEKANANDA.

XLVII

U. S. A.,
9th July, 1895.

. . . About my coming to India, the matter stands thus I am, as your Highness (The Maharaja of Khetri) well knows, a man of dogged perseverance. I have planted a seed in this country; it is already a plant, and I expect it to be a tree very soon. I have got a few hundred followers. I shall make several Sannyâsins, and then I go to India leaving the work to them. The more the Christian priests oppose me, the more I am determined to leave a permanent mark on their country. . . . I have already some friends in London. I am going there by the end of August. . . . This winter anyway has to be spent partly in London and partly in New York, and then I shall be free to go to India. There will be enough men to carry on the work here after this winter if the Lord is kind. Each work has to pass through these stages — ridicule, opposition, and then acceptance. Each man who thinks ahead of his time is sure to be misunderstood. So opposition and persecution are welcome, only I have to be steady and pure and must have immense faith in God, and all these will vanish. . . .

VIVEKANANDA.

XLVIII

C/O MISS DUTCHER,
THOUSAND ISLAND PARK, N. Y.
31st July, 1895.

DEAR FRIEND, (Francis Leggett)

I wrote you before this a letter, but as I am afraid it was not posted carefully, I write another.

I shall be in time before the 14th. I shall have to come to New York before the 11th anyway. So there will be time enough to get ready.

I shall go with you to Paris, for my principal object in going with you is to see *you married*. When you go away for a trip, I go to London. That is all.

It is unnecessary to repeat my everlasting love and blessings for you and yours.

Ever your son,

VIVEKANANDA.

XLIX

U. S. A.,
August 1895.

By the time this reaches you, dear Alasinga, I shall be in Paris. . . . I have done a good deal of work this year and hope to do a good deal more in the next. Don't bother about the missionaries. It is quite natural that they should cry. Who does not when his bread is dwindling away? The missionary funds have got a big gap the last two years, and it is on the increase. However, I wish the missionaries all success. So long as you have love for God and Guru and faith in truth, nothing can hurt you, my son. But the loss of any of these is dangerous. You have remarked well; my ideas are going to work in the West better than in India. . . . I have done more for India than India ever did for me. . . . I believe in truth, the Lord sends me workers by the scores wherever I go — and they are not like the . . . disciples either — they are ready to give up their lives for their Guru. Truth is my God, the universe my country I do not believe in duty. Duty is the curse of the Samsâri (householder), not for the Sannyâsin. Duty is humbug. I am free, my bonds are cut; what care I where this body goes or does not go. You have helped me well right along. The Lord will reward you. I sought praise neither from India nor from America, nor do I seek such bubbles. I have a truth to teach, I, the child of God And He that gave me the truth will send me fellow workers from the earth's bravest and best. You Hindus will see in a few years what the Lord does in the West. You are like the Jews of old — dogs in the manger, who neither eat nor allow others to eat. You have no religion your God is the kitchen, your Bible the cooking-pots. . . . You are a few brave lads. . . . Hold on, boys, no cowards among my children. . . . Are great things ever done smoothly? Time, patience, and indomitable will must show. I could have told you many things that would have made your heart leap, but I will not. I want iron wills and hearts that do not know how to quake. Hold on. The Lord bless you.

Ever yours with blessings,

VIVEKANANDA.

L

THOUSAND ISLAND PARK,
August, 1895.

DEAR MRS. BULL,

. . . Now here is another letter from Mr. Sturdy I send it over to you. See how things are being prepared ahead. Don't you think this coupled with Mr. Leggett's invitation as a divine call? I think so and am following it. I am going by the end of August with Mr. Leggett to Paris, and then I go to London.

What little can be done for my brethren and my work is all the help I want from you now. I have done my duty to my people fairly well. Now for the world that gave me this body — the country that gave me the ideas, the humanity which allows me to be one of them!

The older I grow, the more I see behind the idea of the Hindus that *man* is the greatest of all beings. So say the Mohammedans too. The angels were asked by Allah to bow down to Adam. Iblis did not, and therefore he became Satan. This earth is higher than all heavens; this is the greatest school in the universe; and the Mars or Jupiter people cannot be higher than we, because they cannot communicate with us. The only so-called higher beings are the departed, and these are nothing but men who have taken another body. This is finer, it is true, but still a *man-body*, with hands and feet, and so on. And they live on this earth in another Âkâsha, without being absolutely invisible. They also think, and have consciousness, and everything else like us. So they also are men, so are the Devas, the angels. But man alone becomes *God*; and they all have to become men again in order to become God. . . .

Yours etc.,

VIVEKANANDA.

LI

HOTEL CONTINENTAL,
3 RUE CASTIGLIONE, PARIS,
26th August, 1895.

Aum tat sat

DEAR FRIEND, (Mr. E. T. Sturdy)

I arrived here day before yesterday. I came over to this country as the guest of an American friend who is going to be married here next week.

I shall have to stop here with him till that time; and after that I shall be free to come to London.

Eagerly anticipating the joy of meeting you,

Ever yours in Sat,

VIVEKANANDA.

LII

PARIS,
9th September, 1895.

DEAR ALASINGA,

. . . I am surprised you take so seriously the missionaries' nonsense. . . . If the people in India want me to keep strictly to my Hindu diet, please tell them to send me a cook and money enough to keep him. This silly *bossism* without a mite of real help makes me laugh. On the other hand, if the missionaries tell you that I have ever broken the two great vows of the Sannyâsin — chastity and poverty — tell them that they are *big liars*. Please write to the missionary Hume asking him categorically to write you what misdemeanour he saw in me, or give you the names of his informants, and whether the information was *first-hand or not*; that will settle the question and expose the whole thing. . . .

As for me, mind you, I stand at nobody's dictation. I know my mission in life, and no chauvinism about me; I belong as much to India as to the world, no humbug about that. I have helped you all I could. You must now help yourselves. What country has any special claim on me? Am I any nation's slave? Don't talk any more silly nonsense, you faithless atheists.

I have worked hard and sent all the money I got to Calcutta and Madras, and then after doing all this, stand their silly dictation! Are you not ashamed? What do I owe to them? Do I care a fig for their praise or fear their blame? I am a singular man, my son, not even you can understand me yet. Do your work; if you cannot, stop; but do not try to "boss" me with your nonsense. I *see* a greater Power than man, or God, or devil at my back. I require nobody's help. I have been all my life helping others. . . . They cannot raise a few rupees to help the work of the greatest man their country ever produced — Ramakrishna Paramahamsa; and they talk nonsense and want to dictate to the man for whom they did nothing, find who did everything he could for them! Such is the ungrateful world!

Do you mean to say I am born to live and die one of those caste-ridden, superstitious, merciless, hypocritical, atheistic *cowards* that you find only amongst the educated Hindus? I hate cowardice; I will have nothing to do with cowards or political nonsense. I do not believe in any politics. God and truth are the only politics in the world, everything else is trash.

I am going to London tomorrow. . . .

Yours with blessings

VIVEKANANDA.

LIII

LONDON,
24th October, 1895.

DEAR ALASINGA,

. . . I have already delivered my first address, and you may see how well it has been received by the notice in the *Standard*. The *Standard* is one of the most influential conservative papers. I am going to be in London for a month, then I go off to America and shall come back again next summer. So far you see the seed is well sown in England. . . .

Take courage and work on. Patience and steady work — this is the only way. Go on; remember — patience and purity and courage and steady work. . . . So long as you are pure, and true to your principles, you will never fail — Mother will never leave you, and all blessings will be yours.

Yours with love,

VIVEKANANDA.

LIV

LONDON,
18th November, 1895.

DEAR ALASINGA,

. . . In England my work is really splendid, I am astonished myself at it. The English people do not: talk much in the newspapers, but they work silently. I am sure of more work in England than in America. Bands and bands come, and I have no room for so many; so they squat on the floor, ladies and all. I tell them to imagine that they are under the sky of India, under a spreading banyan, and they like the idea. I shall have to go away next week, and they are so sorry. Some think my work here will be hurt a little if I go away so soon. I do not think so. I do not depend on men or things. The Lord alone I depend upon — and He works through me.

. . . Please everybody without becoming a hypocrite and without being a coward. Hold on to your own ideas with strength and purity, and whatever obstructions may now be in your way, the world is bound to listen to you in the long run. . . .

I have no time even to die, as the Bengalis say. I work, work, work, and earn my own bread and help my country, and this all alone, and then get only criticism from friends and foes for all that! Well, you are but children, I shall have to bear everything. I have sent for a Sannyâsin from Calcutta and shall leave him to work in London. I want one more for America — I want my *own man*. Guru-Bhakti is the foundation of all spiritual development.

. . . I am really tired from incessant work. Any other Hindu would have died if he had to work as hard as I have to. . . . I want to go to India for a long rest. . . .

Ever yours with love and blessings,

VIVEKANANDA.

LV

228 W. 39TH ST., NEW YORK,
20th December, 1895.

DEAR ALASINGA,

. . . Have patience and be faithful unto death. Do not fight among yourselves. Be perfectly pure in money dealings. . . . We will do great things yet. . . . So long as you have faith and honesty and devotion, everything will prosper.

. . . In translating the Suktas, pay particular attention to the Bhâshyakâras (commentators), and pay no attention whatever to the orientalists. They do not understand a single thing about our Shâstras (scriptures). It is not given to dry philologists to understand philosophy or religion. . . . For instance the word Ânid-avâtam in the Rig-Veda was translated — "He lived without breathing". Now, here the reference is really to the chief Prâna, and Avâtam has the root-meaning for unmoved, that is, without vibration. It describes the state in which the universal cosmic energy, or Prana, remains before the Kalpa (cycle of creation) begins: vide — the Bhashyakaras. Explain according to *our* sages and not according to the so-called European scholars. What do they know?

. . . Be bold and fearless, and the road will be clear. . . . Mind, you have nothing whatsoever to do with the Theosophists. If you all stand by me and do not lose patience, I assure you, we shall do great work yet. The great work will be in England, my boy, by and by. I feel you sometimes get disheartened, and I am afraid you get temptations to play in the hands of the Theosophists. Mind you, the Guru-Bhakta will conquer the world — this is the one evidence of history. . . . It is faith that makes a lion of a man. You must always remember how much work I have to do. Sometimes I have to deliver two or three lectures a day — and thus I make my way against all odds — hard work; any weaker man would die.

. . . Hold on with faith and strength; be true, be honest, be pure, and don't quarrel among yourselves. Jealousy is the bane of our race.

With love to you and all our friends there,

Yours,

VIVEKANANDA.

LVI

228 W. 39TH STREET,
NEW YORK,
10th February, 1896.

DEAR SISTER, (Miss Mary Hale)

I was astonished at learning that you have not received my letter yet. I wrote immediately after the receipt of yours and also sent you some booklets of three lectures I delivered in New York. These Sunday public lectures are now taken down in shorthand and printed. Three of them made two little pamphlets, several copies of which I have forwarded to you. I shall be in New York two weeks more, and then I go to Detroit to come back to Boston felt a week or two.

My health is very much broken down this year by constant work. I am very nervous. I have not slept a single night soundly this winter. I am sure I am working too much, yet a big work awaits me in England.

I will have to go through it, and then I hope to reach India and have a rest all the rest of my life. I hale tried at least to do my best for the world, leaving, tile result to the Lord. Now I am longing for rest. Hope I will get some, and the Indian people will give me up. How I would like to become dumb for some years and not talk at all! I was not made for these struggles and fights of the world. I am naturally dreamy and restful. I am a born idealist, can only live in a world of dreams; the very touch of fact disturbs my visions arid makes me unhappy. They, will be done!

I am ever ever grateful to you four sisters; to you I owe everything I have in this country. May you be ever blessed and happy. Wherever I be, you will always be remembered with the deepest gratitude and sincerest love. The whole life is a succession of dreams. My ambition is to be a conscious dreamer, that is all. My love to all — to Sister Josephine.

Ever your affectionate brother,

VIVEKANANDA.

LVII

228 W. 39TH STREET, NEW YORK,
13th February, 1896.

BLESSED AND BELOVED, (E. T. Sturdy)

About the Sannyâsin coming over from India, I am sure he will help you in the translation work, also in other work. Later on, when I come, I may send him over to America. Today another Sannyasin has been added to the list. This time it is a man who is a genuine American and a religious teacher of some standing in the country. He was Dr. Street. He is now Yogananda, as his leaning is all towards Yoga.

I have been sending regular reports to the *Brahmavâdin* from here. They will be published soon. It takes such a long time for things to reach India! Things are growing nobly in India. As there was no hocus-pocus from the beginning, the Vedanta is drawing the attention of the highest classes in American society. Sarah Bernhardt, the French actress, has been playing "Iziel" here. It is a sort of Frenchified life of Buddha, where a courtesan "Iziel" wants to seduce the Buddha, under the banyan - and the Buddha preaches to her the vanity of the world, whilst she is sitting all the time in Buddha's lap. However, all is well that ends well — the courtesan fails. Madame Bernhardt acts the courtesan. I went to see the Buddha business — and Madame spying me in the audience wanted to have an interview with me. A swell family of my acquaintance arranged the affair. There were besides Madame M. Morrel, the celebrated singer, also the great electrician Tesla. Madame is a very scholarly lady and has studied up the metaphysics a good deal. M. Morrel was being interested, but Mr. Tesla was charmed to hear about the Vedantic Prâna and Âkâsha and the Kalpas, which according to him are the only theories modern science can entertain. Now both Akasha and Prana again are produced from the cosmic Mahat, the Universal Mind, the Brahmâ or Ishvara. Mr. Tesla thinks he can demonstrate mathematically that force and matter are reducible to potential energy. I am to go and see him next week, to get this new mathematical demonstration.

In that case, the Vedantic cosmology will be placed on the surest of foundations. I am working a good deal now upon the cosmology and eschatology (That is, doctrine of the last things — death, judgement, etc.) of the Vedanta. I clearly see their perfect unison with modern science, and the elucidation of the one will be followed by that of the other. I intend to write a book later on in the form of questions and answers. (This was never done. But from his lectures in London in 1896, it is easy to see that his mind was still working on these ideas. (See also Vol. VIII Sayings and Utterances & Letter to Mr. Sturdy.)). The first chapter will be on cosmology, showing the harmony between Vedantic theories and modern science.

Brahman = The Absolute

|

Mahat or Ishwara = Primal Creative Energy

Λ

Prana and Akasha = Force and Matter

The eschatology will be explained from the Advaitic standpoint only. That is to say, the dualist claims that the soul after death passes on to the Solar sphere, thence to the Lunar sphere, thence to the Electric sphere. Thence he is accompanied by a Purusha to Brahmaloka. (Thence, says the Advaitist, he goes to Nirvâna.)

Now on the Advaitic side, it is held that the soul neither comes nor goes, and that all these spheres or layers of the universe are only so many varying products of Akasha and Prana. That is to say, the lowest or most condensed is the Solar sphere, consisting of the visible universe, in which Prana appears as physical force, and Akasha as sensible matter. The next is called the Lunar sphere, which surrounds the Solar sphere. This is not the moon at all, but the habitation of the gods, that is to say, Prana appears in it as psychic forces, and Akasha as Tanmâtras or fine particles. Beyond this is the Electric sphere, that is to say, a condition in which the Prana is almost inseparable from Akasha, and you can hardly tell whether Electricity is force or matter. Next is the Brahmaloka. where there is neither Prana nor Akasha, but both are merged in the *mind stuff*, the primal energy. And here — there big neither Prana nor Akasha — the Jiva contemplates the whole universe as Samashti or the sum total of Mahat or mind. This appears as a Purusha, an abstract universal *soul*, yet not the Absolute, for still there is multiplicity. From this the Jiva finds at last that Unity which is the end. Advaitism says that these are the visions which rise in succession before the Jiva, who himself neither goes nor comes, and that in the same way this present vision has been projected. The projection (Srishti) and dissolution must take place in the same order, only one means going backward, and the other coming out.

Now as each individual can only see *his own* universe, that universe is created with his bondage and goes away with his liberation, although it remains for others who are in bondage. Now name and form constitute the universe. A wave in the ocean is a wave, only in so far as it is bound by name and form. If the wave subsides, it is the ocean, but those name and form have immediately vanished for ever. So though the name and form of wave could never be without *water* that was fashioned into the wave by them, yet the name and form themselves were not the wave. They die as soon as ever it returns to water. But other names and forms live in relation to other waves. This name-and-form is called Mâyâ, and the water is Brahman. The wave was nothing but water all the time, yet as a wave it had the name and form. Again this name and form cannot remain for one moment separated from the wave, although the *wave* as water can remain eternally separate from name and form. But because the name and form can never he *separated*, they can never be said to *exist*. Yet they are not *zero*. This is called Maya.

I want to work; all this out carefully, but you will see at a glance that I am on the right track. It will take more study in physiology, on the relations between the higher and lower centres, to fill out the psychology of mind Chitta (mind-stuff), and Buddhi (intellect), and so on. But I have clear light now, free of all hocus-pocus. I want to give them dry, hard reason, softened in tile sweetest syrup of love and made spicy with intense work, and cooked in the kitchen of Yoga, so that even a baby can easily digest it.

Yours etc.,

VIVEKANANDA.

LVIII

U. S. A.,
17th February, 1896.

DEAR ALASINGA,

. . . I have used some very harsh words in my letters, which you ought to excuse, as you know, I get nervous at times. The work is terribly hard; and the more it is growing, the harder it is becoming. I need a long rest very badly. Yet a great work is before me in England.

Have patience, my son — it will grow beyond all your expectations. . . . Every work has got to pass through hundreds of difficulties before succeeding. Those that persevere will see the light, sooner or later.

I have succeeded now in rousing the very heart of the American civilisation, New York, but it has been a terrific struggle. . . . I have spent nearly, all I had on this New York work and in England. Now things are in such a shape that they will go on. Just as I am writing to you, every one of my bones is paining after last afternoon's long Sunday public lecture. Then you see, to put the Hindu ideas into English and then make out of dry philosophy and intricate mythology and queer startling psychology, a religion which shall be easy, simple, popular, and at the same time meet the requirements of the highest minds — is a task only those can understand who have attempted it. The dry, abstract Advaita must become living — poetic — in everyday life; out of hopelessly intricate mythology must come concrete moral forms; and out of bewildering Yogi-ism must come the most scientific and practical psychology — and all this must be put in a form so that a child may grasp it. That is my life's work. The Lord only knows how far I shall succeed. "To work we have the right, not to the fruits thereof." It is hard work, my boy, hard work! To keep one's self steady in the midst of this whirl of Kâma-Kânchana (lust and gold) and hold on to one's own ideals, until disciples are moulded to conceive of the ideas of realisation and perfect renunciation, is indeed difficult work, my boy. Thank God already there is great success. I cannot blame the missionaries and others for not understanding me — they hardly ever saw a man who did not care in the least about women and money. At first they could not believe it to be possible; how could they? You must not think that the Western nations have the same ideas of chastity and purity as the Indians. Their equivalents are virtue and courage. . . . People are now flocking to me. Hundreds have now become convinced that there are men who can really control their bodily desires; and reverence and respect for these principles are growing. All things come to him who waits. May you be blessed for ever and ever!

Yours with love,

VIVEKANANDA.

LIX

BOSTON,
23rd March, 1896.

DEAR ALASINGA,

. . . One of my new Sannyâsins is indeed a woman. . . . The others are men. I am going to make some more in England and take them over to India with me. These "white" faces will have more influence in India than the Hindus; moreover, they are vigorous, the Hindus are *dead*. The only hope of India is from the masses. The upper classes are physically and morally dead. . . .

My success is due to my popular style — the greatness of a teacher consists in the simplicity of his language.

. . . I am going to England next month. I am afraid I have worked too much; my nerves are almost shattered by this long-continued work. I don't want you to sympathise, but only I write this so that you may not expect much from me now. Work on, the best way you can. I have very little hope of being able to do great things now. I am glad, however, that a good deal of literature has been created by taking down stenographic notes of my lectures. Four books are ready. . . . Well, I am satisfied that I have tried my best to do good, and shall have a clear conscience when I retire from work and sit down in a cave.

With love and blessings to all,

VIVEKANANDA.

LX

U. S. A.,
March, 1896.

DEAR ALASINGA,

. . . Push on with the work. I will do all I can. . . . If it pleases the Lord, yellow-garbed Sannyâsins will be common here and in England. Work on, my children.

Mind, so long as you have faith in your Guru, nothing will be able to obstruct your way. That translation of the three Bhâshyas (commentaries) will be a great thing in the eyes of the Westerners.

. . . Wait, my child, wait and work on. Patience, patience. . . . I will burst on the public again in good time. . . .

Yours with love,

VIVEKANANDA.

LXI

NEW YORK,
14th April, 1896.

DEAR DR. NANJUNDA RAO,

I received your note this morning. As I am sailing for England tomorrow, I can only write a few hearty lines. I have every sympathy with your proposed magazine for boys, and will do my best to help it on. You ought to make it independent, following the same lines as the *Brahmavâdin,* only making the style and matter much more popular. As for example, there is a great chance, much more than you ever dream of, for those wonderful stories scattered all over the Sanskrit literature, to be re-written and made popular. That should be the one great feature of your journal. I will write stories, as many as I can, when time permits. Avoid all attempts to make the journal scholarly — the *Brahmavadin* stands for that — and it will slowly make its way all over the world, I am sure. Use the simplest language possible, and you will succeed. The main feature should be the teaching of principles through stories. Don't make it metaphysical at all. As to the business part, keep it wholly in your hands. "Too many cooks spoil the broth." In India the one thing we lack is the power of combination, organisation, the first secret of which is obedience.

I have also promised to help starting a magazine in Bengali in Calcutta. Only the first year I used to charge for my lectures. The last two years, my work was entirely free of all charges. As such, I have almost no money to send you or the Calcutta people. But I will get people to help you with funds very soon. Go on bravely. Do not expect success in a day or a year. Always hold on to the highest. Be steady. Avoid jealousy and selfishness. Be obedient and eternally faithful to the cause of truth, humanity, and your country, and you will move the world. Remember it is the *person*, the life, which is the secret of power — nothing else. Keep this letter and read the last lines whenever you feel worried or jealous. Jealousy is the bane of all slaves. It is the bane of our nation. Avoid that always. All blessings attend you and all success.

Yours affectionately,

VIVEKANANDA.

LXII

ENGLAND,
14th July, 1896.

DEAR DR. NANJUNDA RAO,

The numbers of *Prabuddha Bharata* have been received and distributed too to the class. It is very satisfactory. It will have a great sale, no doubt, in India. In America I may get also a number of subscribers. I have already arranged for advertising it in America and Goodyear has done it already. But here in England the progress will be slower indeed. The great drawback here is — they all want to start papers of their own; and it is right that it should be so, seeing that, after all, no foreigner will ever write the English language as well as the native Englishman, end the ideas, when put in good English, will spread farther than in Hindu English. Then again it is much more difficult to write a story in a foreign language than an essay. I am trying my best to get you subscribers here. But you must not depend on any *foreign help*. Nations, like individuals, must help themselves. This is real patriotism. If a nation cannot do that, its time has not yet come. It must wait. It is from Madras that the new light *must* spread all over India. With this end you must stork. One point I will remark however. The cover is simply barbarous. It is awful and hideous. If it is possible, change it. Make it symbolical and simple, without human figures at all. The banyan tree does not mean awakening, nor does the hill, nor the saint, nor the European couple. The lotus is a symbol of regeneration.

We are awfully behindhand in art especially in that of painting. For instance, make a small scene of spring re-awakening in a forest, showing how the leaves and buds are coming again. Slowly go on, there are hundreds of ideas to be put forward. You see the symbol I made for the *Raja-Yoga*, printed by Longman Green and Co. You can get it at Bombay. It consists of my lectures on Raja-Yoga in New York.

I am going to Switzerland next Sunday, and shall return to London in the autumn, and take up the work again. . . . I want rest very badly, you know.

Yours with all blessings etc.,

VIVEKANANDA.

LXIII

SWITZERLAND,
6th August, 1896.

DEAR ALASINGA,

I learnt from your letter the bad financial state the *Brahmavâdin* is in. I will try to help you when I go back to London. You must not lower the tone. Keep up the paper. Very soon I will be able to help you in such a manner as to make you free of this nonsense teacher business. Do not be afraid. Great things are going to be done, my child. Take heart. The *Brahmavadin* is a jewel — it must not perish. Of course, such a paper has to be kept up by private help always, and *we will do it*. Hold on a few months more.

Max Müller's article on Shri Ramakrishna has been published in the *Nineteenth Century*. I will send you a copy as soon as I get it. He writes me very nice letters and wants material for a big work on Ramakrishna's life. Write to Calcutta to send all the material they can to Max Müller.

I have received the communication to the American paper before. You must not publish it in India. Enough of this newspaper blazoning, I am tired of it anyhow. Let us go our own way, and let fools talk. Nothing can resist truth.

I am, as you see, now in Switzerland and am always on the move. I cannot and must not do anything in the way of writing, nor much reading either. There is a big London work waiting for me from next month. In winter I am going back to India and will try to set things on their feet there.

My love to all. Work on, brave hearts, fail not — no saying nay; work on — the Lord is behind the work. Mahâshakti is with you.

Yours with love and blessings,

VIVEKANANDA.

PS. Do not be afraid, money and everything will come soon.

V.

LXIV

SWITZERLAND,
8th August, 1896.

DEAR ALASINGA,

Since writing to you a few days ago I have found my way to let you know that I am in a position to do this for the *Brahmavadin*. I will give you Rs. 100 a month for a year or two, i.e. £60 or £70 a year, i.e. as much as would cover Rs. 100 a month. That will set you free to work for the *Brahmavadin* and make it a better success. Mr. Mani Iyer and a few friends can help in raising fund that would cover the printing etc. What is the income from subscription? Can these be employed to pay the contributors and get a fine series of articles? It is not necessary that everybody should understand all that is written in the *Brahmavadin*, but that they must subscribe from patriotism and good Karma — the Hindus I mean.

Several things are necessary. First there should be strict integrity. Not that I even hint that any of you would digress from it, but the Hindus have a peculiar slovenliness in business matters, not being sufficiently methodical and strict in keeping accounts etc.

Secondly, entire devotion to the cause, knowing that your SALVATION depends upon making the *Brahmavadin* a success. Let this paper be your Ishtadevata, and then you will see how success comes. I have already sent for Abhedânanda from India. I hope there will be no delay with him as it was with the other Swami. On receipt of this letter you send me a clear account of all the income and the expenses of the *Brahmavadin* so that I may judge from it what best can be done. Remember that perfect purity, disinterestedness, and obedience to the Guru are the secret of all success. . . .

A big foreign circulation of a religious paper is impossible. It must be supported by the Hindus if they have any sense of virtue or gratitude left to them.

By the by, Mrs. Annie Besant invited me to speak at her Lodge, on Bhakti. I lectured there one night. Col. Olcott also was there. I did it to show my sympathy for all sects. . . . Our countrymen must remember that in things of the Spirit we are the teachers, and not foreigners — but in things of the world we ought to learn from them.

I have read Max Müller's article, which is a good one, considering that when he wrote it, six months ago, he had no material except Mazoomdar's leaflet. Now he writes me a long and nice letter offering to write a book on Shri Ramakrishna. I have already supplied him with much material, but a good deal more is needed from India.

Work on! Hold on! Be brave! Dare anything and everything!

. . . It is all misery, this Samsâra, don't you see!

Yours with blessings and love,

VIVEKANANDA.

LXV

LUCERNE,
23rd August, 1896.

BLESSED AND BELOVED, (E. T. Sturdy)

Today I received a letter from India written by Abhedânanda that in all probability he had started on the 11th August by the B.I.S.N., "S.S.Mombassa". He could not get an earlier steamer; else he would have started earlier. In all probability he would be able to secure a passage on the Mombassa. The Mombassa will reach London about the 15th of September. As you already know, Miss Müller changed the date of my visiting Deussen to the 19th September. I shall not be in London to receive Abhedananda. He is also coming without any warm clothing; but I am afraid by that time it will begin to cool in England, and he will require at least some underwear and an overcoat. You know all about these things much better than I. So kindly keep a look out for this Mombassa. I expect also another letter from him.

I am suffering from a very bad cold indeed. I hope by this time Mohin's money from the Raja has arrived to your care. If so, I do not want the money I gave him back. You may give him the whole of it.

I had some letters from Goodwin and Sâradânanda. They are doing well. Also one from Mrs. Bull regretting that you and I could not be corresponding members of some Society, she is founding at Cambridge. I do remember to have written to her about your and my non-acquiescence in this membership. I have not yet been able to write even a line. I had not a moment's time even to read, climbing up hill and going down dale all the time. We will have to begin the march again in a few days. Kindly give my love to Mohin and Fox when you see them next.

With love to all our friends,

Yours ever,

VIVEKANANDA.

LXVI

SWITZERLAND,
26th August, 1896.

DEAR NANJUNDA RAO,

I have just now got your letter. I am on the move. I have been doing a great deal of mountain-climbing and glacier-crossing in the Alps. Now I am going to Germany. I have an invitation from Prof. Deussen to visit him at Kiel. From thence I go back to England. Possibly I will return to India this winter.

What I objected to in the design for the *Prabuddha Bhârata* was not only its tawdriness, but the crowding in of a number of figures without any purpose. A design should be simple, symbolical, and condensed. I will try to make a design for *Prabuddha Bharata* in London and send it over to you. . . .

The work is going on beautifully, I am very glad to say. . . . I will give you one advice however. All combined efforts in India sink under the weight of one iniquity — we have not yet developed strict business principles. Business is business, in the highest sense, and no friendship — or as the Hindu proverb says "eye-shame" — should be there. One should keep the clearest account of everything in one's charge — and never, never apply the funds intended for one thing to any other use whatsoever — even if one starves the next moment. This is business integrity. Next, energy unfailing. Whatever you do let that be your worship for the time. Let this paper be your God for the time, and you will succeed.

When you have succeeded in this paper, start vernacular ones on the same lines in Tamil, Telugu, Canarese, etc. We must reach the masses. The Madrasis are good, energetic, and all that, but the land of Shankarâchârya has lost the spirit of renunciation, it seems.

My children must plunge into the breach, must renounce the world — then the firm foundation will be laid.

Go on bravely — never mind about designs and other details at present — "With the horse will come the reins". Work unto death — I am with you, and when I am gone, my spirit will work with you. This life comes and goes — wealth, fame, enjoyments are only of a few days. It is better, far better to die on the field of duty, preaching the truth, than to die like a worldly worm. Advance!

Yours with all love and blessings,

VIVEKANANDA.

LXVII

C/O MISS H. MÜLLER,
AIRLIE LODGE, RIDGEWAY GARDENS,
WIMBLEDON, ENGLAND,
22nd September, 1896.

DEAR ALASINGA,

I am sure you have got the article on Ramakrishna, I sent you, by Max Müller. Do not be sorry, he does not mention me there at all, as it was written six months before he knew me. And then who cares whom he mentions, if he is right in the main point. I had a beautiful time with Prof. Deussen in Germany. Later, he and I came together to London, and we have already become great friends.

I am soon sending you an article on him. Only pray do not put that old-fashioned "Dear Sir" before my articles. Have you seen the Râja-Yoga book yet? I will try to send you a design for the coming year. I send you a *Daily News* article on a book of travel written by the Czar of Russia. The paragraph in which he speaks of India as the land of spirituality and wisdom, you ought to quote in your paper and send the article to the *Indian Mirror*.

You are very welcome to publish the Jnâna-Yoga lectures, as well as Dr. (Nanjunda Rao) in his *Awakened India* — only the simpler ones. They have to be very carefully gone through and all repetitions and contradictions taken out. I am sure I will now have more time to write. Work on with energy.

With love to all.

Yours,

VIVEKANANDA.

PS. I have marked the passage to be quoted, the rest of course is useless for a paper.

I do not think it would be good just now to make the paper a monthly one yet, unless you are sure of giving a good bulk. As it is now, the bulk and the matter are all very poor. There is yet a vast untrodden field, namely — the writing of the lives and works of Tulasidâsa, Kabir, Nânak, and of the saints of Southern India. They should be written in a thorough-going, scholarly style, and not in a slipshod, slovenly way. In fact, the ideal of the paper, apart from the preaching of Vedanta, should be to make it a magazine of Indian research and scholarship, of course, bearing on religion. You must approach the best writers and get carefully-written articles from their pen. Work on with all energy.

Yours with love,

VIVEKANANDA.

LXVIII

14 GREY COAT GARDENS,
WESTMINSTER, LONDON.
1896

DEAR ALASINGA,

I have returned about three weeks from Switzerland but could not write you further before. I have sent you by last mail a paper on Paul Deussen of Kiel. Sturdy's plan about the magazine is still hanging fire. As you see, I have left the St. George's Road place. We have a lecture hall at 39 Victoria Street. C/o E. T. Sturdy will always reach me for a year to come. The rooms at Grey Coat Gardens are only lodgings for self and the other Swami taken for three mouths only. The work in London is growing apace, the classes are becoming bigger as they go on. I have no doubt this will go on increasing at this rate and the English people are steady and loyal. Of course, as soon as I leave, most of this fabric will tumble down. Something will happen. Some strong man will arise to take it up. The Lord knows what is good. In America there is room for twenty preachers on the Vedanta and Yoga. Where to get these preachers and where also the money to bring them? Half the United States can be conquered in ten years, given a number of strong and genuine men. Where are they? We are all boobies over there! Selfish cowards, with our nonsense of lip-patriotism, orthodoxy, and boasted religious feeling! The Madrasis have more of go and steadiness, but every fool is married. Marriage! Marriage! Marriage! . . . Then the way our boys are married nowadays! . . . It is very good to aspire to be a nonattached householder; but what we want in Madras is not that just now — but non-marriage. . . .

My child, what I want is muscles of iron and nerves of steel, inside which dwells a mind of the same material as that of which the thunderbolt is made. Strength, manhood, Kshatra-Virya Brahma-Teja. Our beautiful hopeful boys — they have everything, only if they are not slaughtered by the millions at the altar of this brutality they call marriage. O Lord, hear my wails! Madras will then awake when at least one hundred of its very heart's blood, in the form of its educated young men, will stand aside from the world, gird their loins, and be ready to fight the battle of truth, marching on from country to country. One blow struck outside of India is equal to a hundred thousand struck within. Well, all will come if the Lord wills it.

Miss Müller was the person who offered that money I promised. I have told her about your new proposal. She is thinking about it. In the meanwhile I think it is better to give her some work. She has consented to be the agent for the *Brahmavadin* and *Awakened India*. Will you write to her about it? Her address is Airlie Lodge, Ridgeway Gardens, Wimbledon, England. I was living with her over there for the last few weeks. But the London work cannot go on without my living in London. As such I have changed quarters. I am sorry it has chagrined Miss Müller a bit. Cannot help. Her full name is Miss Henrietta Müller. Max Müller is getting very friendly. I am soon going to deliver two lectures at Oxford.

I am busy writing something big on the Vedanta philosophy. I am busy collecting passages from the various Vedas bearing on the Vedanta in its threefold aspect. You can help me by getting someone to collect passages bearing on, first the Advaitic idea, then the Vishishtâdvaitic, and the Dvaitic from the Samhitâs, the Brâhmanas, the Upanishads, and the Purânas. They should be classified and very legibly written with the name and chapter of the book, in each case. It would be a pity to leave the West without leaving something of the philosophy in book form.

There was a book published in Mysore in Tamil characters, comprising all the one hundred and eight Upanishads; I saw it in Professor Deussen's library. Is there a reprint of the same in Devanâgari? If so, send me a copy. If not, send me the Tamil edition, and also write on a sheet the Tamil letters and compounds, and all juxtaposed with its Nagari equivalents, so that I may learn the Tamil letters.

Mr. Satyanathan, whom I met in London the other day, said that there has been a friendly review of my Râja-Yoga book in the *Madras Mail*, the chief Anglo-Indian paper in Madras. The leading physiologist in America, I hear, has been charmed with my speculations. At the same time, there have been some in England, who ridiculed my ideas. Good! My speculations of course are awfully bold; a good deal of them will ever remain meaningless; but there are hints in it which the physiologists had better taken up earlier. Nevertheless, I am quite satisfied with the result. "Let them talk badly of me if they please, but let them talk", is my motto.

In England, of course, they are gentlemen and never talk the rot I had in America. Then again the English missionaries you see over there are nearly all of them from the dissenters. They are not from the gentleman class in

England. The gentlemen here, who are religious; all belong to the English Church. The dissenters have very little voice in England and no education. I never hear of those people here against whom you time to time warn me. They are unknown here and dare not talk nonsense. I hope Ram K. Naidu is already in Madras, and you are enjoying good health.

Persevere on, my brave lads. We have only just begun. Never despond! Never say enough! . . . As soon as a man comes over to the West and sees different nations, his eyes open. This way I get strong workers — not by talking, but by practically showing what we have in India and what we have not. I wish at least that a million Hindus had travelled all over the world!

Yours ever with love,

VIVEKANANDA.

LXIX

C/O E. T. STURDY, ESQ.,
39 VICTORIA STREET, LONDON,
28th October, 1896.

DEAR ALASINGA,

. . . I am not yet sure what month I shall reach India. I will write later about it. The new Swami (Swami Abhedananda) delivered his maiden speech yesterday at a friendly society's meeting. It was good and I liked it; he has the making of a good speaker in him, I am sure.

. . . You have not yet brought out the — . . Again, books must be cheap for India to have a large sale; the types must be bigger to satisfy the public. . . . You can very well get out a cheap edition of — if you like. I have not reserved any copyright on it purposely. You have missed a good opportunity by not getting out the — book earlier, but we Hindus are so slow that when we have done a work, the opportunity has already passed away, and thus we are the losers. Your — book came out after a year's talk! Did you think the Western people would wait for it till Doomsday? You have lost three-fourths of the sale by this delay. . . . That Haramohan is a fool, slower than you, and his printing is diabolical. There is no use in publishing books that way; it is cheating the public, and should not be done. I shall most probably return to India accompanied by Mr. and Mrs. Sevier, Miss Müller, and Mr. Goodwin. Mr. and Mrs. Sevier are probably going to settle in Almora at least for some time, and Goodwin is going to become a Sannyâsin. He of course will travel with me. It is he to whom we owe all our books. He took shorthand notes of my lectures, which enabled the books to be published. . . . All these lectures were delivered on the spur of the moment, without the least preparation, and as such, they should be carefully revised and edited. . . .Goodwin will have to live with me. . . . He is a strict vegetarian.

Yours with love,

VIVEKANANDA.

PS. I have sent a little note to the *Indian Mirror* today about Dr. Barrows and how he should be welcomed. You also write some good words of welcome for him in the *Brahmavadin*. All here send love.

V.

LXX

LONDON,
28th October, 1896.

(On the eve of the lecture-tour of Dr. Barrows in India at the end of 1896, Swami Vivekananda in a letter to the *Indian Mirror,* Calcutta, introduced the distinguished visitor to his countrymen and advised them to give him a fitting reception. He wrote among other things as follows:)

Dr. Barrows was the ablest lieutenant Mr. C. Boney could have selected to carry out successfully his great plan of the Congresses at the World's Fair, and it is now a matter of history how one of these Congresses scored a unique distinction under the leadership of Dr. Barrows.

It was the great courage, untiring industry, unruffled patience, and never-failing courtesy of Dr. Barrows that made the Parliament a grand success.

India, its people, and their thoughts have been brought more prominently before the world than ever before by that wonderful gathering at Chicago, and that national benefit we certainly owe to Dr. Barrows more than to any other man at that meeting.

Moreover, he comes to us in the sacred name of religion, in the name of one of the great teachers of mankind, and I am sure, his exposition of the system of the Prophet of Nazareth would be extremely liberal and elevating. The Christ-power this man intends to bring to India is not that of the intolerant, dominant superior, with heart full of contempt for everything else but its own self, but that of a brother who craves for a brother's place as a co-worker of the various powers already working in India. Above all, we must remember that gratitude and hospitality are the peculiar characteristics of Indian humanity; and as such, I would beg my countrymen to behave in such a manner that this stranger from the other side of the globe may find that in the midst of all our misery, our poverty, and degradation, the heart beats as warm as of yore, when the "wealth of Ind" was the proverb of nations and India was the land of the "Aryas".

LXXI

14 GREY COAT GARDENS,
WESTMINSTER, S. W.,
11th November, 1896.

DEAR ALASINGA,

I shall most probably start on the 16th of December, or may be a day or two later. I go from here to Italy, and after seeing a few places there, join the steamer at Naples. Miss Müller, Mr. and Mrs. Sevier, and a young man called Goodwin are accompanying me. The Seviers are going to settle at Almora. So is Miss Müller. Sevier was an officer in the Indian army for 5 years. So he knows India a good deal. Miss Müller was a Theosophist who adopted Akshay. Goodwin is an Englishman, through whose shorthand notes it has been possible for the pamphlets to be published.

I arrive at Madras first from Colombo. The other people go their way to Almora. I go from thence direct to Calcutta. I will write you the exact information when I start.

Yours affly.,

VIVEKANANDA.

PS. The first edition of *Râja-Yoga* is sold out, and a second is in the press. India and America are the biggest buyers.

V.

LXXII

39 VICTORIA STREET,
LONDON, S. W.,
20th November, 1896.

DEAR ALASINGA,

I am leaving England on the 16th of December for Italy, and shall catch the North German Lloyd S. S. Prinz Regent Luitpold at Naples. The steamer is due at Colombo on the 14th of January next.

I intend to see a little of Ceylon, and shall then go to Madras. I am being accompanied by three English friends — Capt. and Mrs. Sevier and Mr. Goodwin. Mr. Sever and his wife are going to start a place near Almora in the Himalayas which I intend to make my Himalayan Centre, as well as a place for Western disciples to live as Brahmachârins and Sannyâsins. Goodwin is an unmarried young man who is going to travel and live with me, he is like a Sannyasin.

I am very desirous to reach Calcutta before the birthday festival of Shri Ramakrishna. . . . My present plan of work is to start two centres, one in Calcutta and the other in Madras, in which to train up young preachers. I have funds enough to start the one in Calcutta, which being the scene of Shri Ramakrishna's life-work, demands my first attention. As for the Madras one, I expect to get funds in India.

We will begin work with these three centres; and later on, we will get to Bombay and Allahabad. And from these points, if the Lord is pleased, we will invade not only India, but send over bands of preachers to every country in the world. That should be our first duty. Work on with a heart. 39 Victoria will be the London headquarters for some time to come, as the work will be carried on there. Sturdy had a big box of *Brahmavâdin* I did not know before. He is now canvassing subscribers for it.

Now we have got one Indian magazine in English fixed. We can start some in the vernaculars also. Miss M. Noble of Wimbledon is a great worker. She will also canvass for both the Madras papers. She will write you. These things will grow slowly but surely. Papers of this kind are supported by a small circle of followers. Now they cannot be expected to do too many things at a time — they have to buy the books, find the money for the work in England, subscribers for the paper here, and then subscribe to Indian papers. It is too much. It is more like trading than teaching. Therefore you must wait, and yet I am sure there will be a few subscribers here. Again, there must be work for the people here to do when I am gone, else the whole thing will go to pieces. Therefore there must be a paper here, so also in America by and by. The Indian papers are to be supported by the Indians. To make a paper equally acceptable to all nationalities means a staff of writers from all nations; and that means at least a hundred thousand rupees a year.

You must not forget that my interests are *international* and not Indian alone. I am in good health; so is Abhedananda.

With all love and blessings,

VIVEKANANDA.

LXXIII

LONDON,
13th December, 1896.

DEAR MADAM, (An American lady.)

We have only to grasp the idea of gradation of morality and everything becomes clear.

Renunciation — non-resistance — non-destructiveness — are the ideals to be attained through less and less worldliness, less and less resistance, less and less destructiveness. Keep the ideal in view and work towards it. None can live in the world without resistance, without destruction, without desire. The world has not come to that state yet when the ideal can be realised in society.

The progress of the world through all its evils making it fit for the ideals, slowly but surely. The majority will have to go on with this slow growth — the exceptional ones will have to get out to realise the idea in the present state of things.

Doing the duty of the time is the best way, and if it is done only as a duty, it does not make us attached.

Music is the highest art and, to those who understand is the highest worship.

We must try our best to destroy ignorance and evil. Only we have to learn that evil is destroyed by the growth of good.

Yours faithfully,

VIVEKANANDA.

LXXIV

(Translated from Bengali)

ॐ तत् सत्

ROSE BANK,

THE MAHARAJA OF BURDWAN'S HOUSE,

DARJEELING,

6th April, 1897.

HONOURED MADAM, (Shrimati Sarala Ghoshal — Editor, *Bharati*)

I feel much obliged for the *Bhârati* sent by you, and consider myself fortunate that the cause, to which my humble life has been dedicated, has been able to win the approbation off highly talented ladies like you.

In this battle of life, men are rare who encourage the initiator off new thought, not to speak of women who would offer him encouragement, particularly in our unfortunate land. It is therefore that the approbation of an educated Bengali lady is more valuable than the loud applause of all the men of India.

May the Lord grant that many women like you be born in this country, and devote their lives to the betterment of their motherland!

I have something to say in regard to the article you have written about me in the *Bharati*. It is this. It has been for the good of India that religious preaching in the West has been and will be done. It has ever been my conviction that we shall not be able to rise unless the Western people come to our help. In this country no appreciation of merit can yet be found, no financial strength, and what is most lamentable of all, there is not a bit of practicality.

There are many things to be done, but means are wanting in this country. We have brains, but no hands. We have the doctrine of Vedanta, but we have not the power to reduce it into practice. In our books there is the doctrine of universal equality, but in work we make great distinctions. It was in India that unselfish and disinterested work of the most exalted type was preached but in practice *we* are awfully cruel, awfully heartless — unable to think of anything besides our own mass-of-flesh bodies.

Yet it is only through the present state of things that it is possible to proceed to work. There is no other way. Every one has the power to judge of good end evil, but he is the hero who undaunted by the waves of Samsâra — which is full of errors, delusions, and miseries — with one hand wipes the tears, and with the other, unshaken, shows the path of deliverance. On the one hand there is the conservative society, like a mass of inert matter; on the other the restless, impatient, fire-darting reformer; the way to good lies between the two. I heard in Japan that it was the belief of the girls of that country that their dolls would be animated if they were loved with all their heart. The Japanese girl never breaks her doll. O you of great fortune! I too believe that India will awake again if anyone could love with all his heart the people of the country — bereft of the grace of affluence, of blasted fortune, their discretion totally lost, downtrodden, ever-starved, quarrelsome, and envious. Then only will India awake, when hundreds of large-hearted men and women, giving up all desires of enjoying the luxuries of life, will long and exert themselves to their utmost for the well-being of the millions of their countrymen who are gradually sinking lower and lower in the vortex of destitution and ignorance. I have experienced even in my insignificant life that good motives, sincerity, and infinite love can conquer the world. One single soul possessed of these virtues can destroy the dark designs of millions of hypocrites and brutes.

My going to the West again is yet uncertain; if I go, know that too will be for India. Where is the strength of men in this country? Where is the strength of money? Many men and women of the West are ready to do good to India by serving even the lowest Chandâlas, in the Indian way, and through the Indian religion. How many such are there in this country? And financial strength! To meet the expenses or my reception, the people of Calcutta made me deliver a lecture and sold tickets! . . . I do not blame nor censure anybody for this, I only want to show that our well-being is impossible without men and money coming from the West.

Ever grateful and ever praying to the Lord for your welfare,

VIVEKANANDA.

LXXV

ALMORA,
29th May, 1897.

MY DEAR DOCTOR SHASHI (BHUSHAN GHOSH),

Your letter and the two bottles containing the medicines were duly received. I have begun from last evening a trial of your medicines. Hope the combination will have a better effect than the one alone.

I began to take a lot of exercise on horseback, both morning and evening. Since that I am very much better indeed. I was so much better the first week of my gymnastics that I have scarcely felt so well since I was a boy and used to have kusti (wrestling) exercises. I really began to feel that it was a pleasure to have a body. Every movement made me conscious of strength — every movement of the muscles was pleasurable. That exhilarating feeling has subsided somewhat, yet I feel very strong. In a trial of strength I could make both G. G. and Niranjan go down before me in a minute. In Darjeeling I always felt that I was not the same man. Here I feel that I have no disease whatsoever, but there is one marked change. I never in my life could sleep as soon as I got into bed. I must toss for at least two hours. Only from Madras to Darjeeling (during the first month) I would sleep as soon as my head touched the pillow. That ready disposition to sleep is gone now entirely, and my old tossing habit and feeling hot after the evening meal have come back. I do not feel any heat after the day meal. There being an orchard here, I began to take more fruit than usual as soon as I came. But the only fruit to be got here now is the apricot. I am trying to get more varieties from Naini Tâl. There has not been any thirst even though the days are fearfully hot. . . . On the whole my own feeling is one of revival of great strength and cheerfulness, and a feeling of exuberant health, only I am afraid I am getting fat on a too much milk diet. Don't you listen to what Yogen writes. He is a hypochondriac himself and wants to make everybody so. I ate one-sixteenth of a barphi (sweetmeat) in Lucknow, and that according to Yogen was what put me out of sorts in Almora! Yogen is expected here in a few days. I am going to take him in hand. By the by, I am very susceptible to malarious influences. The first week's indisposition at Almora might have been caused to a certain extent by my passage through the Terai. Anyhow I feel very, very strong now. You ought to see me, Doctor, when I sit meditating in front of the beautiful snow-peaks and repeat from the Upanishads:

न तस्य रोगो न जरा न मृत्युः प्राप्तस्य योगाग्निमयं शरीरम्

— He has neither disease, nor decay, nor death; for, verily, he has obtained a body full of the fire of Yoga."

I am very glad to learn of the success of the meetings of the Ramakrishna Mission at Calcutta. All blessings attend those that help in the great work. . . .

With all love,

Yours in the Lord,

VIVEKANANDA.

LXXVI

ALMORA,
1st June, 1897.

DEAR MR.—,

The objections you show about the Vedas would be valid if the word Vedas meant Samhitâs. The word Vedas includes the three parts, the Samhitas, the Brâhmanas, and the Upanishads, according to the universally received opinion in India. Of these, the first two portions, as being the ceremonial parts, have been nearly put out of sight; the Upanishads have alone been taken up by all our philosophers and founders of sects.

The idea that the Samhitas are the only Vedas is very recent and has been started by the late Swâmi Dayânanda. This opinion has not got any hold on the orthodox population.

The reason of this opinion was that Swami Dayananda thought he could find a consistent theory of the whole, based on a new interpretation of the Samhitas, but the difficulties remained the same, only they fell back on the Brahmanas. And in spite of the theories of interpretation and interpolation a good deal still remains.

Now if it is possible to build a consistent religion on the Samhitas, it is a thousand times more sure that a very consistent and harmonious faith can be based upon the Upanishads, and moreover, here one has not to go against the already received national opinion. Here all the Âchâryas (Teachers) of the past would side with you, and you have a vast scope for new progress.

The Gita no doubt has already become the Bible of Hinduism, and it fully deserves to be so; but the personality of Krishna has become so covered with haze that it is impossible today to draw any life-giving inspiration from that *life*. Moreover, the present age requires new modes of thought and new life.

Hoping this will help you in thinking along these lines.

I am yours with blessings,

VIVEKANANDA.

LXXVII

अलमोड़ा ।

ॐ नमो भगवते रामकृष्णाय ।

यस्य वीर्येण कृतिनो वयं च भुवनानि च ।
रामकृष्णं सदा वन्दे शर्वं स्वतन्त्रमीश्वरम् ॥

"प्रभवति भगवान् विधि" रित्यागमिनः अप्रयोगनिपुणाः प्रयोगनिपुणाश्च पौरुषं बहुमन्यमानाः । तयोः पौरुषेयापौरुषेयप्रतिकारबलयोः विवेकाग्रहनिबन्धनः कलह इति मत्वा यतस्वायुष्मन् शरच्चन्द्र आक्रमितुम् ज्ञानगिरिगुरोर्गरिष्ठं शिखरम् ।

यदुक्तं "तत्त्वनिकषग्रावा विपदिति" उच्येत तदपि शतशः "तत्त्वमसि" तत्त्वाधिकारे । इदमेव तन्निदानं वैराग्यरुजः । धन्यं कस्यापि जीवनं तल्लक्षणाक्रान्तस्य । अरोचिष्णु अपि निर्दिशामि पदं प्राचीनं — "कालः कश्चित् प्रतीक्ष्यताम्" इति । समारूढक्षेपणीक्षेपणश्रमः विश्राम्यतां तन्निर्भरः । पूर्वाहितो वेगः पारं नेष्यति नावम् । तदेवोक्तं —"तत् स्वयं योगसंसिद्धः कालेनात्मनि विन्दति," "न कर्मणा न प्रजया धनेन त्यागेनैके अमृतत्वमानशुः" इत्यत्र त्यागेन वैराग्यमेव लक्ष्यते । तद्वैराग्यं वस्तुशून्यं वस्तुभूतं वा । प्रथमं यदि, न तत्र यतेन कोऽपि कीटभक्षितमस्तिष्केन विना, यद्यपरं, तदेदम् आपतति —त्यागः मनसः संकोचनम् अन्यस्मात् वस्तुनः, पिण्डीकरणं च ईश्वरे वा आत्मनि । सर्वेश्वरस्तु व्यक्तिविशेषो भवितुं नार्हति, समष्टिरित्येव ग्रहणीयम् । आत्मेति वैराग्यवतो जीवात्मा इति नापद्यते, परन्तु सर्वगः सर्वान्तर्यामी सर्वस्यात्मरूपेणावस्थितः सर्वेश्वर एव लक्ष्यीकृतः । स तु समष्टिरूपेण सर्वेषां प्रत्यक्षः । एवं सति जीवेश्वरयोः स्वरूपतः अभेदभावात् तयोः सेवाप्रेमरूपकर्मणोरभेदः । अयमेव विशेषः— जीवे जीवबुद्ध्या या सेवा समर्पिता स दया, न प्रेम, यदात्मबुद्ध्या जीवः सेव्यते, तत् प्रेम । आत्मनो हि प्रेमास्पदत्वं श्रुतिस्मृतिप्रत्यक्षप्रसिद्धत्वात् । तत् युक्तमेव यदवादीत् भगवान् चैतन्यः— प्रेम ईश्वरे, दया जीवे इति । द्वैतवादित्वात् तत्र भगवतः सिद्धान्तः जीवेश्वरयोर्भेदविज्ञापकः समीचीनः । अस्माकं अद्वैतपराणां जीवबुद्धिर्बन्धनाय इति । तदस्माकं प्रेम एव शरणं, न दया । जीवे प्रयुक्तः दयाशब्दोऽपि साहसिकजल्पित इति मन्यामहे । वयं न दयामहे, अपि तु सेवामहे, नानुकम्पानुभूतिरस्माकम्, अपि तु प्रेमानुभवः स्वानुभवः सर्वस्मिन् ।

सैव सर्ववैषम्यसाम्यकरी भवव्याधिनीरुजकरी प्रपञ्चावश्यम्भाव्यत्रितापहरणकरी सर्ववस्तुस्वरूपप्रकाशकरी मायाध्वान्तविध्वंसकरी आब्रह्मस्तम्बपर्यन्त स्वात्मरूपप्रकटनकरी प्रेमानुभूतिर्वैराग्यरूपा भवतु ते शर्मणे शर्मन् ।

इत्यनुदिवसं प्रार्थयति त्वयि धृतचिरप्रेमबन्धः

विवेकानन्दः ।

TRANSLATION

ALMORA,
3rd July, 1897.

Constant salutation be to Shri Ramakrishna, the Free, the Ishvara, the Shiva-form, by whose power we and the whole world are blessed.

Mayest thou live long, O Sharat Chandra! (Sharat Chandra Chakravarty, a disciple of Swamiji.)

Those writers of Shâstra who do not tend towards work say that all-powerful destiny prevails; but others who are workers consider the will of man as superior. Knowing that the quarrel between those who believe in the human will as the remover of misery and others who rely on destiny is due to indiscrimination — try to ascend the highest peak of knowledge.

It has been said that adversity is the touchstone of true knowledge, and this may be said a hundred times with regard to the truth: "Thou art That." This truly diagnoses the Vairâgya (dispassion) disease. Blessed is the life of one who has developed this symptom. In spite of your dislike I repeat the old saying: "Wait for a short time." You are tired with rowing; rest on your oars. The momentum will take the boat to the other side. This has been said in the Gita (IV. 38), "In good time, having reached perfection in Yoga, one realises That in one's own heart;" and in the Upanishad, "Neither by rituals, nor by progeny, nor by riches, but by renunciation alone a few (rare) people attained immortality" (Kaivalya, 2). Here, by the word renunciation Vairagya is referred to. It may be of two kinds, with or without purpose. If the latter, none but worm-eaten brains will try for it. But if the other is referred to, then renunciation would mean the withdrawal of the mind from other things and concentrating it on God or Atman. The Lord of all cannot be any particular individual. He must be the sum total. One possessing Vairagya does not understand by Atman the individual ego but the All-pervading Lord, residing as the Self and Internal Ruler in all. He is perceivable by all as the sum total. This being so, as Jiva and Ishvara are in essence the same, serving the Jivas and loving God must mean one and the same thing. Here is a peculiarity: when you serve a Jiva with the idea that he is a Jiva, it is Dayâ (compassion) and not Prema (love); but when you serve him with the idea that he is the Self, that is Prema. That the Atman is the one objective of love is known from Shruti, Smriti, and direct perception. Bhagavân Chaitanya was right, therefore, when he said, "Love to God and compassion to the Jivas". This conclusion of the Bhagavan, intimating differentiation between Jiva and Ishvara, was right, as He was a dualist. But for us, Advaitists, this notion of Jiva as distinct from God is the cause of bondage. Our principle, therefore, should be love, and not compassion. The application of the word compassion even to Jiva seems to me to be rash and vain. For us, it is not to pity but to serve. Ours is not the feeling of compassion but of love, and the feeling of Self in all.

For thy good, O Sharman, may thine be Vairagya, the feeling of which is love, which unifies all inequalities, cures the disease of Samsâra, removes the threefold misery, inevitable in this phenomenal world, reveals the true nature of all things, destroys the darkness of Mâyâ, and which brings out the Selfhood of everything from Brahma to the blade of grass!

This is the constant prayer of

VIVEKANANDA.

Ever bound to thee in love.

LXXVIII

ALMORA,
9th July, 1897.

DEAR SISTER, (Miss Mary Hale.)

I am very sorry to read between the lines the desponding tone of your letter, and I understand the cause; thank you for your warning, I understand your motive perfectly. I had arranged to go with Ajit Singh to England; but the doctors not allowing, it fell thorough. I shall be so happy to learn that Harriet has met him. He will be only too glad to meet any of you.

I had also a lot of cuttings from different American papers fearfully criticising my utterances about American women and furnishing me with the strange news that I had been outcasted! As if I had any caste to lose, being a Sannyâsin!

Not only no caste has been lost, but it has considerably shattered the opposition to sea-voyage — my going to the West. If I should have to be outcasted, it would be with half the ruling princes of India and almost all of educated India. On the other hand, a leading Raja of the caste to which I belonged before my entering the order got up a banquet in mid honour, at which were most of the *big bugs* of that caste. The Sannyasins, on the other hand, may not dine with any one in India, as it would be beneath the dignity of gods to dine with mere mortals. They are regarded as Nârâyanas, while the others are mere men. And dear Mary, these feet have been washed and wiped and worshipped by the descendants of kings, and there has been a progress through the country which none ever commanded in India.

It will suffice to say that the police were necessary to keep order if I ventured out into the street! That is outcasting indeed! Of course, that took the starch out of the missionaries, and who are they here? — Nobodies. We are in blissful ignorance of their existence all the time. I had in a lecture said something about the missionaries and the origin of that species except the English Church gentlemen, and in that connection had to refer to the very churchy women of America and their power of inventing scandals. This the missionaries are parading as an attack on American women *en masse* to undo my work there, as they well know that anything said against themselves will rather please the U.S. people. My dear Mary, supposing I had said all sorts of fearful things against the "Yanks" — would that be paying off a millionth part of what they say of our *mothers* and *sisters*? "Neptune's waters" would be perfectly useless to wash off the hatred the Christian "Yanks" of both sexes bear to us "heathens of India" — and what harm have we done them? Let the "Yanks" learn to be patient under criticism and then criticise others. It is a well-known psychological fact that those who are ever ready to abuse others cannot bear the slightest touch of criticism from others. Then again, what do I owe them? Except your family, Mrs. Bull, the Leggetts, and a few other kind persons, who else has been kind to me? Who came forward to help me work out my ideas? I had to work till I am at death's door and had to spend nearly the whole of that energy in America, so that the Americans may learn to be broader and more spiritual. In England I worked only six months. There was not a breath of scandal save one, and that was the working of an American woman, which greatly relieved my English friends — not only no attacks but many of the best English Church clergymen became my firm friends, and without asking I got much help for my work, and I am sure to get much more. There is a society watching my work and getting help for it, and four respectable persons followed me to India to help my work, and dozens were ready, and the next time I go, hundreds will be.

Dear, dear Mary, do not be afraid for me. . . The world is big, very big, and there must be some place for me even if the "Yankees" rage. Anyhow, I am quite satisfied with my work. I never planned anything. I have taken things as they came. Only one idea was burning in my brain — to start the machine for elevating the Indian masses — and that I have succeeded in doing to a certain extent. It would have made your heart glad to see how my boys are working in the midst of famine and disease and misery — nursing by the mat-bed of the cholera stricken Pariah and feeding the starving Chandâla — and the Lord sends help to me and to them all. "What are men?" He is with me, the Beloved, He was when I was in America, in England, when I was roaming about unknown from place to place in India. What do I care about what they talk — the babies, they do not know any better. What! I, who have realised the Spirit and the vanity of all earthly nonsense, to be swerved from my path by babies' prattle! Do I look like that?

I had to talk a lot about myself because I owned that to you. I feel my task is done — at most three or four years more of life are left. I have lost all wish for my salvation. I never wanted earthly enjoyments. I must see my machine in strong working order, and then knowing sure that I have put in a lever for the good of humanity, in India at least, which no power can drive back, I will sleep, without caring what will be next; and may I be born again and again, and suffer thousands of miseries so that I may worship the only

God that exists, the only God I believe in, the sum total of all souls — and above all, my God the wicked, my God the miserable, my God the poor of all races, of all species, is the special object of my worship.

"He who is in you and is outside of you, who works through every hand, who walks through every foot, whose body you are, Him worship, and break all other idols.

"He who is the high and the low, the saint and the sinner, the god and the worm, Him worship, the visible, the knowable, the real, the omnipresent, break all other idols.

"In whom there is neither past life nor future birth, nor death nor going or coming, in whom we always have been and always will be one, Him worship, break all other idols.

"Ay, fools, neglecting the living Gods and His infinite reflection with which the world is full, and running after, imaginary shadows! Him worship, the only visible, and break all other idols."

My time is short. I have got to unbreast whatever I have to say, without caring if it smarts some or irritates others. Therefore, my dear Mary, do not be frightened at whatever drops from my lips, for the power behind me is not Vivekananda but He the Lord, and He knows best. If I have to please the world, that will be injuring the world; the voice of the majority is wrong, seeing that they govern and make the sad state of the world. Every new thought must create opposition — in the civilised a polite sneer, in the vulgar savage howls and filthy scandals.

Even these earthworms must stand erect, even children must see light. The Americans are drunk with new wine. A hundred waves of prosperity have come and gone over my country. We have learned the lesson which no child can yet understand. It is vanity. This hideous world is Maya. Renounce and be happy. Give up the idea of sex and possessions. There is no other bond. Marriage and sex and money the only living devils. All earthly love proceeds from the body. No sex, no possessions; as these fall off, the eyes open to spiritual vision. The soul regains its own infinite power. How I wish I were in England to see Harriet. I have one wish left — to see you four sisters before I die, and that must happen.

Yours ever affly.,

VIVEKANANDA.

LXXIX

ALMORA,
28th July, 1897.

MY DEAR MOTHER, (Mrs. Leggett.)

Many many thanks for your beautiful and kind letter. I wish I were in London to be able to accept the invitation with the Raja of Khetri. I had a great many dinners to attend in London last season. But it was fated not to be, and my health did not permit my going over with the Raja.

So Alberta is once more at home in America. I owe her a debt of gratitude for all she did for me in Rome. How is Holli? To both of them my love, and kiss the new baby for me, my youngest sister.

I have been taking some rest in the Himalayas for nine months. Now I am going down to the plains to be harnessed once more for work.

To Frankincense and Joe Joe and Mabel my love, and so to you eternally.

Yours ever in the Lord,

VIVEKANANDA.

LXXX

THE MATH, BELUR,
11th August, 1897.

DEAR JOE, (Miss MacLeod.)

. . . Well, the work of the Mother will not suffer; because it has been built and up to date maintained upon truth, sincerity, and purity. Absolute sincerity has been its watchword.

Yours with all love,

VIVEKANANDA.

LXXXI

MURREE,
11th October, 1897.

MY DEAR JAGAMOHANLAL,

. . . Leave words when you start for Bombay to somebody to take care of three Sannyasins I am sending to Jaipur. Give them food and good lodging. They will be there till I come. They are fellows — innocent, not learned. They belong to me, and one is my Gurubhâi (brother-disciple). If they like, take them to Khetri where I will come soon. I am travelling now quietly. I will not even lecture much this year. I have no more faith in all this noise and humbug which brings no practical good. I must make a silent attempt to start my institution in Calcutta; for that I am going to visit different centres quietly to collect funds.

Yours with blessings,
VIVEKANANDA.

LXXXII

DEHRA DUN,
24th November, 1897.

MY DEAR M.,

Many many thanks for your second leaflet (leaves from the *Gospel*). It is indeed wonderful. The move is quite original, and never was the life of a great Teacher brought before the public untarnished by the writer's mind, as you are presenting this one. The language also is beyond all praise, so fresh, so pointed, and withal so plain and easy.

I cannot express in adequate terms how I have enjoyed the leaflets. I am really in a transport when I read them. Strange, isn't it? Our Teacher and Lord was so original, and each one of us will have to be original or nothing. I now understand why none of us attempted his life before. It has been reserved for you, this great work. He is with you evidently.

With all love and Namaskâra,

VIVEKANANDA.

PS. The Socratic dialogues are Plato all over; you are entirely hidden. Moreover, the dramatic part is infinitely beautiful. Everybody likes it here and in the West.

LXXXIII

ALMORA,
9th June, 1898.

YOUR HIGHNESS, (Maharaja of Khetri.)

Very sorry to learn that you are not in perfect health. Sure you will be in a few days.

I am starting for Kashmir on Saturday next. I have your letter of introduction to the Resident, but better still if you kindly drop a line to the Resident telling him that you have already given an introduction to me.

Will you kindly ask Jagamohan to write to the Dewan of Kishangarh reminding him of his promise to supply me with copies of Nimbârka Bhâshya on the *Vyâsa-Sutras* and other Bhashyas (commentaries) through his Pandits.

With all love and blessings,

Yours,

VIVEKANANDA.

PS. Poor Goodwin is dead. Jagamohan knows him well. I want a couple of tiger skins, if I can, to be sent to the Math as present to two European friends. These seem to be most gratifying presents to Westerners.

LXXXIV

C/O RISIBAR MOOKERJEE,
CHIEF JUDGE,
KASHMIR,
17th September, 1898.

YOUR HIGHNESS, (Maharaja of Khetri.)

I have been very ill here for two weeks. Now getting better. I am in want of funds. Though the American; friends are doing everything they can to help me, I feel shame to beg from them all the time, especially as illness makes one incur contingent expenses. I have no shame; to beg of one person in the world and that is yourself. Whether you give or refuse, it is the same to me. If possible send some money kindly. How are you? I am going down by the middle of October.

Very glad to learn from Jagamohan the complete recovery of the Kumar (Prince) Saheb. Things are going on well with me; hoping it is the same with you.

Ever yours in the Lord,
VIVEKANANDA.

LXXXV

LAHORE,
16th October, 1898.

YOUR HIGHNESS, (Maharaja of Khetri.)

The letter that followed my wire gave the desired information; therefore I did not wire back about my health in reply to yours.

This year I suffered much in Kashmir and am now recovered and going to Calcutta direct today. For the last ten years or so I have not seen the Puja of Shri Durgâ in Bengal which is the great affair there. I hope this year to be present.

The Western friends will come to see Jaipur in a week or two. If Jagamohan be there, kindly instruct him to pay some attention to them and show them over the city and the old arts.

I leave instructions with my brother Saradananda to write to Munshiji before they start for Jaipur.

How are you and the Prince? Ever as usual praying for your welfare,

I remain yours affectionately,

VIVEKANANDA.

PS. My future address is Math, Belur, Howrah Dist. Bengal.

LXXXVI

MATH, BELUR,
HOWRAH DIST., BENGAL,
26th October, 1898.

YOUR HIGHNESS, (Maharaja of Khetri.)

I am very very anxious about your health. I had a great desire to look in on my way down, but my health failed completely, and I had to run down in all haste. There is some disturbance with my heart, I am afraid.

However I am very anxious to know about your health. If you like I will come over to Khetri to see you. I am praying day and night for your welfare. Do not lose heart if anything befalls, the "Mother" is your protection. Write me all about yourself. . . . How is the Kumar Saheb?

With all love and everlasting blessings,

Ever yours in the Lord,

VIVEKANANDA.

LXXXVII

THE MATH, BELUR,
HOWRAH DIST.,
November (?), 1898.

YOUR HIGHNESS, (Maharaja of Khetri.)

Very glad to learn that you and the Kumar are enjoying good health As for me, my heart has become very weak. Change, I do not think, will do me any good, as for the last 14 years I do not remember to have stopped at one place for 3 months at a stretch. On the other hand if by some chance I can live for months in one place, I hope it will do me good. I do not mind this. However, I feel that my work in this life is done. Through good and evil, pain and pleasure, my life-boat has been dragged on. The one great lesson I was taught is that life is misery, nothing but misery. Mother knows what is best. Each one of us is in the hands of Karma; it works itself out — and no nay. There is only one element in life which is worth having at any cost, and it is love. Love immense and infinite, broad as the sky and deep as the ocean — this is the one great gain in life. Blessed is he who gets it.

Ever yours in the Lord,

VIVEKANANDA.

LXXXVIII

MATH, BELUR,
15th December, 1898.

YOUR HIGHNESS, (Maharaja of Khetri.)

Your very kind letter received with the order of 500 on Mr. Dulichand. I am a little better now. Don't know whether this improvement will continue or not.

Are you to be in Calcutta this winter, as I hear? Many Rajas are coming to pay their respects to the new Viceroy. The Maharaja of Sikar is here, I learn from the papers already.

Ever praying for you and yours,

Yours in the Lord,

VIVEKANANDA.

LXXXIX

(Translated from Bengali)

DEOGHAR, VAIDYANATH.
3rd January, 1899.

DEAR MOTHER, (Shrimati Mrinalini Bose)

Some very important questions have been raised in your letter. It is not possible to answer them fully in a short note, still I reply to them as briefly as possible.

(1) Rishi, Muni, or God — none has power to force an institution on society. When the needs of the times press hard on it, society adopts certain customs for self-preservation. Rishis have only recorded those customs As a man often resorts even to such means as are good for immediate self-protection but which are very injurious in the future, similarly society also not unfrequently saves itself for the time being, but these immediate means which contributed to its preservation turn out to be terrible in the long run.

For example, take the prohibition of widow-marriage in our country. Don't think that Rishis or wicked men introduced the law pertaining to it. Notwithstanding the desire of men to keep women completely under their control, they never could succeed in introducing those laws without betaking themselves to the aid of a social necessity of the time. Of this custom two points should be specially observed:

(a) Widow-marriage takes place among the lower classes.

(b) Among the higher classes the number of women is greater than that of men.

Now, if it be the rule to marry every girl, it is difficult enough to get one husband apiece; then how to get, in succession, two or three for each? Therefore has society put one party under disadvantage, i.e. it does not let her have a second husband, who has had one; if it did, one maid would have to go without a husband. On the other hand, widow-marriage obtains in communities having a greater number of men than women, as in their case the objection stated above does not exist. It is becoming more and more difficult in the West, too, for unmarried girls to get husbands.

Similar is the case with the caste system and other social customs.

So, if it be necessary to change any social custom the *necessity* underlying it should be found out first of all, and by altering it, the custom will die of itself. Otherwise no good will be done by condemnation or praise.

(2) Now the question is: Is it for the good of the public at large that social rules are framed or society is formed? Many reply to this in the affirmative; some, again, may hold that it is not so. Some men, being comparatively powerful, slowly bring all others under their control and by stratagem, force, or adroitness gain their own objects. If this be true, what can be the meaning of the statement that there is danger in giving liberty to the ignorant? What, again, is the meaning of liberty?

Liberty does not certainly mean the absence of obstacles in the path of misappropriation of wealth etc. by you and me, but it is our natural right to be allowed to use our own body, intelligence, or wealth according to our will, without doing any harm to others; and all the members of a society ought to have the same opportunity for obtaining wealth, education, or knowledge. The second question is: Those who say that if the ignorant and the poor be given liberty, i.e. full right to their body, wealth, etc., and if their children have the same opportunity to better their condition and acquire knowledge as those of the rich and the highly situated, they would become perverse — do they say this for the good of society or blinded by their selfishness? In England too I have heard, "Who will serve us if the lower classes get education?"

For the luxury of a handful of the rich, let millions of men and women remain submerged in the hell of want and abysmal depth of ignorance, for if they get wealth and education, society will be upset!

Who constitute society? The millions — or you, I, and a few others of the upper classes?

Again, even if the latter be true, what ground is there for our vanity that we lead others? Are we omniscient? " उद्धरेदात्मनात्मानं — One should raise the self by the self." Let each one work out one's own salvation. Freedom in all matters, i.e. advance towards Mukti is the worthiest gain of man. To advance oneself towards freedom — physical, mental, and spiritual — and help others to do so, is the supreme prize of man. Those social rules which stand in the way of the unfoldment of this freedom are injurious, and steps should be taken to destroy them speedily. Those institutions should be encouraged by which men advance in the path of freedom.

That in this life we feel a deep love at first sight towards a particular person who may not be endowed with extraordinary qualities, is explained by the thinkers of our country as due to the associations of a past incarnation.

Your question regarding the will is very interesting: it is the subject to know. The essence of all religions is the annihilation of desire, along with which comes, of a certainty, the annihilation of the will as well, for desire is only the name of a particular mode of the will. Why, again, is this world? Or why are these manifestations of the will? Some religions hold that the evil will should be destroyed and not the good. The denial of desire here would be compensated by enjoyments hereafter. This reply does not of course satisfy the wise. The Buddhists, on the other hand, say that desire is the cause of misery, its annihilation is quite desirable. But like killing a man in the effort to kill the mosquito on his cheek, they have gone to the length of annihilating their own selves in their efforts to destroy misery according to the Buddhistic doctrine.

The fact is, what we call will is an inferior modification of something higher. Desirelessness means the disappearance of the inferior modification in the form of will and the appearance of that superior state That state is beyond the range of mind and intellect. But though the look of the gold mohur is quite different from that of the rupee and the pice, yet as we know for certain that the gold mohur is greater than either, so, that highest state — Mukti, or Nirvâna, call it what you like — though out of the reach of the mind and intellect, is greater than the will and all other powers. It is no power, but power is its modification, therefore it is higher. Now you will see that the result of the proper exercise of the will, first with motive for an object and then without motive, is that the will-power will attain a much higher state.

In the preliminary state, the form of the Guru is to be meditated upon by the disciple. Gradually it is to be merged in the Ishta. By Ishta is meant the object of love and devotion. . . . It is very difficult to superimpose divinity on man, but one is sure to succeed by repeated efforts. God is in every man, whether man knows it or not; your loving devotion is bound to call up the divinity in him.

Ever your well-wisher,

VIVEKANANDA.

XC

THE MATH, BELUR,
HOWRAH, BENGAL,
2nd February, 1899.

MY DEAR JOE, (Miss Josephine MacLeod.)

You must have reached N.Y. by this time and are in the midst of your own after a long absence. Fortune has favoured you at every step of this journey — even the sea was smooth and calm, and the ship nearly empty of undesirable company. Well, with me it is doing otherwise. I am almost desperate I could not accompany you. Neither did the change at Vaidyanath do me any good. I nearly died there, was suffocating for eight days and nights!! I was brought back to Calcutta more dead than alive, and here I am struggling to get back to life again.

Dr. Sarkar is treating me now.

I am not so despondent now as I was. I am reconciled to my fate. This year seems to be very hard for us. Yogananda, who used to live in Mother's house, is suffering for the last month and every day is at death's door. Mother knows best. I am roused to work again, though not personally but am sending the boys all over India to make a stir once more. Above all, as you know, the chief difficulty is of funds. Now that you are in America, Joe, try to raise some funds for our work over here.

I hope to rally again by March, and by April I start for Europe. Again Mother knows best.

I have suffered mentally and physically all my life, but Mother's kindness has been immense. The joy and blessings I had infinitely more than I deserve. And I am struggling not to fail Mother, but that she will always find me fighting, end my last breath will be on the battlefield.

My best love and blessings for you ever and ever.

Ever yours in the Truth,

VIVEKANANDA.

XCI

THE MATH,
ALAMBAZAR (?),
14th June, 1899.

MY DEAR FRIEND, (Raja of Khetri.)

I want your Highness in that fashion as I am here, you need most of friendship and love just now.

I wrote you a letter a few weeks ago but could not get news of yours. Hope you are in splendid health now. I am starting for England again on the 20th this month.

I hope also to benefit somewhat by this sea-voyage.

May you be protected from all dangers and may all blessings ever attend you!

I am yours in the Lord,

VIVEKANANDA.

PS. To Jagamohan my love and good-bye.

XCII

RIDGELY,
2nd September, 1899.

DEAR —,

. . . Life is a series of fights and disillusionments. . . . The secret of life is not enjoyment, but education through experience. But, alas, we are called off the moment we begin really to learn. That seems to be a potent argument for a future existence. . . . Everywhere it is better to have a whirlwind come over the work. That clears the atmosphere and gives us a true insight into the nature of things. It is begun anew, but on adamantine foundations. . . .

Yours with best wishes,

VIVEKANANDA.

XCIII

(Translated from Bengali)

MATH, BELUR,
26th December, 1900.

DEAR SHASHI, (Swami Ramakrishnananda)

I got all the news from your letter. If your health is bad, then certainly you should not come here; and also I am going to Mayavati tomorrow. It is absolutely necessary that I should go there once.

If Alasinga comes here, he will have to await my return. I do not know what those here are deciding about Kanai. I shall return shortly from Almora, and then I may be able to visit Madras. From Vaniyambadi I have received a letter. Write to the people there conveying my love and blessings, and tell them that on my way to Madras I shall surely visit them. Give my love to all. Don't work too hard. All is well here.

Yours affectionately,

VIVEKANANDA.

XCIV

PRABUDDHA BHARATA OFFICE,
ADVAITA ASHRAMA,

MAYAVATI (VIA ALMORA),
KUMAON, HIMALAYAS,
6th January, 1901.

MY DEAR MOTHER, (Mrs. Ole Bull.)

I send you forthwith a translation of the *Nâsadiya* Hymn sent by Dr. Bose through you. I have tried to make it as literal as possible.

I hope Dr. Bose has recovered his health perfectly by this time.

Mrs. Sevier is a strong woman, and has borne her loss quietly and bravely. She is coming over to England in April, and I am going over with her.

I ought to come to England as early as I can this summer; and as she must go to attend to her husband's affairs, I accompany her.

This place is very, very beautiful, and they have made it simply exquisite. It is a huge place several acres in area, and is very well kept. I hope Mrs. Sevier will be in a position to keep it up in the future. She wishes it ever so much, of course.

My last letter from Joe informed me that she was going up the . . . with Mme Calvé.

I am very glad to learn that Margot is leaving her lore for future use. Her book has been very much appreciated here, but the publishers do not seem to make any effort at sale.

The first day's touch of Calcutta brought the asthma back; and every night I used to get a fit during the two weeks I was there. I am, however, very well in the Himalayas.

It is snowing heavily here, and I was caught in a blizzard on the way; but it is not very cold, and all this exposure to the snows for two days on my way here seems to have done me a world of good.

Today I walked over the snow uphill about a mile, seeing Mrs. Sevier's lands; she has made beautiful roads all over. Plenty of gardens, fields, orchards, and large forests, all in her land. The living houses are so simple, so clean, and so pretty, and above all so suited for the purpose.

Are you going to America soon? If not, I hope to see you in London in three months.

Kindly give my best wishes to Miss Olcock and kindly convey my undying love to Miss Müller the next time you see her; so to Sturdy. I have seen my mother, my cousin, and all my people in Calcutta.

Kindly send the remittance you send my cousin to me — in my name so that I shall cash the cheque and give her the money. Saradananda and Brahmananda and the rest were well in the Math when I last left them.

All here send love.

Ever your loving son,

VIVEKANANDA.

PS. Kali has taken two sacrifices; the cause has already two European martyrs. Now, it is going to rise up splendidly.

V.

My love to Alberta and Mrs. Vaughan.

The snow is lying all round six inches deep, the sun is bright and glorious, and now in the middle of the day we are sitting outside, reading. And the snow all about us! The winter here is very mild in spite of the snow. The air is dry and balmy, and the water beyond all praise.

V.

XCV

MAYAVATI,
HIMALAYAS,
15th January, 1901.

MY DEAR STURDY,

I learn from Saradananda that you have sent over Rs. 1,529-5-5 to the Math, being the money that was in hand for work in England. I am sure it will be rightly used.

Capt. Sevier passed away about three months ago. They have made a fine place here in the mountains and Mrs. Sevier means to keep it up. I am on a visit to her, and I may possibly come over to England with her.

I wrote you a letter from Paris. I am afraid you did not get it.

So sorry to learn the passing away of Mrs. Sturdy. She has been a very good wife and good mother, and it is not ordinarily one meets with such in this life.

This life is full of shocks, but the effects pass away anyhow, that is the hope.

It is not because of your free expression of opinion in your last letter to me that I stopped writing. I only let the wave pass, as is my wont. Letters would only have made a wave of a little bubble.

Kindly tender my regards and love to Mrs. Johnson and other friends if you meet them.

And I am ever yours in the Truth,

VIVEKANANDA.

XCVI

THE MATH, BELUR,
HOWRAH DIST.,
BENGAL,
26th January, 1901.

MY DEAR MOTHER, (Mrs. Ole Bull)

Many thanks for your very encouraging words. I needed them very much just now. The gloom has not lifted with the advent of the new century, it is visibly thickening. I went to see Mrs. Sevier at Mayavati. On my way I learnt of the sudden death of the Raja of Khetri. It appears he was restoring some old architectural monument at Agra, at his own expense, and was up some tower on inspection. Part of the tower came down, and he was instantly killed.

The three cheques have arrived. They will reach my cousin when next I see her.

Joe is here, but I have not seen her yet.

The moment I touch Bengal, especially the Math, the asthmatic fits return! The moment I leave, I recover!

I am going to take my mother on pilgrimage next week. It may take months to make the complete round of pilgrimages. This is the one great wish of a Hindu widow. I have brought only misery to my people all my life. I am trying at least to fulfil this one wish of hers.

I am so glad to learn all that about Margot; everybody here is eager to welcome her back.

I hope Dr. Bose has completely recovered by this time.

I had a beautiful letter also from Mrs. Hammond. She is a great soul.

However, I am very calm and self-possessed this time and find everything better than I ever expected.

With all love,

Ever your son,

VIVEKANANDA.

XCVII

MATH, BELUR

MY DEAR SHASHI, (Swami Ramakrishnananda)

I am going with my mother to Rameswaram, that is all. I don't know whether I shall go to Madras at all. If I go, it will be strictly private. My body and mind are completely worked out; I cannot stand a single person. I do not want anybody. I have neither the strength nor the money, nor the will to take up anybody with me. Bhaktas (devotees) of Guru Maharaj or not, it does not matter. It was very foolish of you even to ask such a question. Let me tell you again, I am more dead than alive, and strictly refuse to see anybody. If you cannot manage this, I don't go to Madras. I have to become a bit selfish to save my body.

Let Yogin-Ma and others go their own way. I shall not take up any company in my present state of health.

Yours in love,

VIVEKANANDA.

XCVIII

THE MATH, BELUR,
HOWRAH DIST., BENGAL,
2nd February, 1901.

MY DEAR MOTHER, (Mrs. Ole Bull)

Several days ago I received your letter and a cheque for Rs. 150 included. I will tear up this one, as the three previous cheques I have handed over to my cousin.

Joe is here, and I have seen her twice; she is busy visiting. Mrs. Sevier is expected here soon *en route* to England. I expected to go to England with her, but as it now turns out, I must go on a long pilgrimage with my mother.

My health suffers the moment I touch Bengal; anyhow, I don't much mind it now; I am going on well and so do things about me.

Glad to learn about Margot's success, but, says Joe, it is not financially paying; there is the rub. Mere continuance is of little value, and it is a far cry from London to Calcutta. Well, Mother knows. Everybody is praising Margot's *Kali the Mother*; but alas! they can't get a book to buy; the booksellers are too indifferent to promote the sale of the book.

That this new century may find you and yours in splendid health and equipment for a yet greater future is and always has been the prayer of your son.

VIVEKANANDA.

XCIX

BELUR MATH,
DIST. HOWRAH,
14th February, 1901.

MY DEAR JOE (Miss Josephine MacLeod.)

I am ever so glad to hear that Bois is coming to Calcutta. Send him immediately to the Math. I will be here. If possible I will keep him here for a few days and then let him go again to Nepal.

Yours etc.,

VIVEKANANDA.

C

THE MATH, BELUR,
HOWRAH, BENGAL,
17th February, 1901.

DEAR JOE, (Miss Josephine MacLeod.)

Just now received your nice long letter. I am so glad that you met and approve Miss Cornelia Sorabji. I knew her father at Poona, also a younger sister who was in America. Perhaps her mother will remember me as the Sannyasin who used to live with the Thakore Sahib of Limbdi at Poona.

I hope you will go to Baroda and see the Maharani.

I am much better and hope to continue so for some time. I have just now a beautiful letter from Mrs. Sevier in which she writes a whole lot of beautiful things about you.

I am so glad you saw Mr. Tata and find him so strong and good.

I will of course accept an invitation if I am strong enough to go to Bombay.

Do wire the name of the steamer you leave by for Colombo. With all love,

Yours affectionately,
VIVEKANANDA.

CI

DACCA,
29th March, 1901.

MY DEAR MOTHER, (Mrs. Ole Bull.)

By this time you must have received my other note from Dacca. Saradananda has been suffering badly from fever in Calcutta, which has become simply a hell of demons this year. He has recovered and is now in the Math which, thank God, is one of the healthiest places in our Bengal.

I do not know what conversation took place between you and my mother; I was not present. I suppose it was only an eager desire on her part to see Margot, nothing else.

My advice to Margot would be to mature her plans in England and work them out a good length before she comes back. Good solid work must wait.

Saradananda expects to go to Darjeeling to Mrs. Banerji, who has been in Calcutta for a few days, as soon as he is strong enough.

I have no news yet of Joe from Japan. Mrs. Sevier expects to sail soon. My mother, aunt, and cousin came over five days ago to Dacca, as there was a great sacred bath in the Brahmaputra river. Whenever a particular conjunction of planets takes place, which is very rare, a huge concourse of people gather on the river on a particular spot. This year there has been more than a hundred thousand people; for miles the river was covered with boats.

The river, though nearly a mile broad at the place, was one mass of mud! But it was firm enough, so we had our bath and Pujâ (worship), and all that.

I am rather enjoying Dacca. I am going to take my mother and the other ladies to Chandranath, a holy place at the easternmost corner of Bengal.

I am rather well and hope you and your daughter and Margot are also enjoying splendid health.

With everlasting love,

Ever your son,

VIVEKANANDA.

PS. My cousin and mother send you and Margot their love.

PS. I do not know the date.

V.

CII

THE MATH,
15th May, 1901.

MY DEAR SWARUP (ÂNANDA),

Your letter from Naini Tal is quite exciting. I have just returned from my tour through East Bengal and Assam. As usual I am quite tired and broken down.

If some real good comes out of a visit to H. H. of Baroda I am ready to come over, otherwise I don't want to undergo the expense and exertion of the long journey Think it well over and make inquiries, and write me if you still think it would be best for the Cause for me to come to see H. H. . . .

Yours with love and blessings,

VIVEKANANDA.

CIII

THE MATH, BELUR,
HOWRAH DIST.,
BENGAL, INDIA,
18th May, 1901.

MY DEAR MARY, (Miss Mary Hale.)

Sometimes it is hard work to be tied to the shoestrings of a great name. And that was just what happened to my letter. You wrote on the 22nd January, 1901. You tied me to the latchet of a great name, Miss MacLeod. Consequently the letter has been following her up and down the world. Now it reached me yesterday from Japan, where Miss MacLeod is at present. Well, this, therefore, is the solution of the sphinx's riddle. "Thou shalt not join a great name with a small one."

So, Mary, you have been enjoying Florence and Italy, and I do not know where you be by this time. So, fat old "laidy", I throw this letter to the mercy of Monroe & Co., 7 rue Scribe.

Now, old "laidy" — so you have been dreaming away in Florence and the Italian lakes. Good; your poet objects to its being empty though.

Well, devoted sister, how about myself ? I came to India last fall, suffered all through winter, and went this summer touring through Eastern Bengal and Assam — through a land of giant rivers and hills and malaria — and after hard work of two months had a collapse, and am now back to Calcutta slowly recovering from the effects of it.

The Raja of Khetri died from a fall a few months ago. So you see things are all gloomy with me just now, and my own health is wretched. Yet I am sure to bob up soon and am waiting for the next turn.

I wish I were in Europe, just to have a long chat with you, and then return as quick to India; for, after all, I feel a sort of quiet nowadays, and have done with three-fourths of my restlessness.

My love to Harriet Woolley, to Isabel, to Harriet McKindley; and to mother my eternal love and gratitude. Tell mother, the subtle Hindu's gratitude runs through generations.

Ever yours in the Lord,

VIVEKANANDA.

PS. Write a line when you feel like it.

V.

CIV

(Translated from Bengali)

MATH, BELUR,
DIST., HOWRAH,
3rd June, 1901.

MY DEAR SHASHI, (Swami Ramakrishnanada)

Reading your letter I felt like laughing, and also rather sorry. The cause of the laughter is that you had a dream through indigestion and made yourself miserable, taking it to be real. The cause of my sorrow is that it is clear from this that your health is not good, and that your nerves require rest very badly.

Never have I laid a curse on you, and why should I do so now? All your life you have known my love for you, and today are you doubting it? True, my temper was ever bad, and nowadays owing to illness it occasionally becomes terrible — but know this for certain that my love can never cease.

My health nowadays is becoming a little better. Have the rains started in Madras? When the rains begin a little in the South, I may go to Madras via Bombay and Poona. With the onset of the rains the terrible heat of the South will perhaps subside.

My great love to you and all others. Yesterday Sharat returned to the Math from Darjeeling — his health is much better than it was before. I have come here after a tour of East Bengal and Assam. All work has its ups and downs, its periods of intensity and slackness. Again it will rise up. What fear? . . . .

Whatever that may be, I say that you stop your work for some time and come straight back to the Math. After you have taken a month's rest here, you and I together will make a grand tour via Gujarat, Bombay, Poona, Hyderabad, Mysore to Madras. Would not that be grand? If you cannot do this, stop your lectures in Madras for a month. Take a little good food and sleep well. Within two or three months I shall go there. In any case, reply immediately as to what you decide to do.

Yours with blessings,

VIVEKANANDA.

CV

THE MATH, BELUR,
HOWRAH DIST.,
14th June, 1901.

DEAR JOE, (Miss Josephine MacLeod.)

I am so glad you are enjoying Japan — especially Japanese art. You are perfectly correct in saying that we will have to learn many things from Japan. The help that Japan will give us will be with great sympathy and respect, whereas that from the West unsympathetic and destructive. Certainly it is very desirable to establish a connection between India and Japan.

As for me, I was thrown *hors de combat* in Assam. The climate of the Math is just reviving me a bit. At Shillong — the hill sanatorium of Assam — I had fever, asthma, increase of albumen, and my body swelled to almost twice ills normal size. These symptoms subsided, however, as soon as I reached the Math. It is dreadfully hot this year; but a bit of rain has commenced, and I hope we will soon have the monsoon in full force. I have no plans just now, except that the Bombay Presidency wants me so badly that I think of going there soon. We are thinking of starting touring through Bombay in a week or so.

The 300 dollars you speak of sent by Lady Betty have not reached me yet, nor have I any intimation of its arrival from General Patterson.

He, poor man, was rather miserable, after his wife and children sailed for Europe and asked me to come and see him, but unfortunately I was so ill, and am so afraid of going into the City that I must wait till the rains have set in.

Now, Joe dear, if I am to go to Japan, this time it is necessary that I take Saradananda with me to carry on the work. Also I must have the promised letter to Li Huang Chang from Mr. Maxim; but Mother knows the rest. I am still undecided.

So you went to Alanquinan to see the foreteller? Did he convince you of his powers? What did he say? Write particular *s'il vous plait*.

Jules Bois went as far as Lahore, being prevented from entering Nepal. I learn from the papers that he could not bear the heat and fell ill; then he took ship *et bon voyage*. He did not write me a single line since we met in the Math. You also are determined to drag Mrs. Bull down to Japan from Norway all the way — *bien, Mademoiselle, vous êtes use puissante magicienne, sans doute*. (Well, Miss, you are undoubtedly a powerful magician.). Well, Joe, keep health and spirits up; the Alanquinan man's words come out true most of them; and *glorie et honneur* await you — and Mukti. The natural ambition of woman is through marriage to climb up, leaning upon a man; but those days are gone. You shall be great without the help of any man, just as you are, plain, dear Joe — our Joe, everlasting Joe. . . .

We have seen enough of this life to care for any of its bubbles have we not Joe? For months I have been practicing to drive away all sentiments; therefore I stop here, and good-bye just now. It is ordained by Mother we work together; it has been already for the good of many; it shall be for the good of many more; so let it be. It is useless planning, useless high flights; Mother will find Her own way; . . . rest assured.

Ever yours with love and heart's blessings,

VIVEKANANDA.

PS. Just now came a cheque for Rs. 300 from Mr. Okakura, and the invitation. It is very tempting, but Mother knows all the same.

V.

CVI

THE MATH, BELUR,
18th June, 1901.

DEAR JOE, (Miss Josephine MacLeod.)

I enclose with yours an acknowledgement of Mr. Okakura's money — of course I am up to all your tricks.

However, I am really trying to come, but you know — one month to go — one to come — and a few days' stay! Never mind, I am trying my best. Only my terribly poor health, some legal affairs, etc., etc., may make a little delay.

With everlasting love,
VIVEKANANDA.

CVII

THE MATH, BELUR,
HOWRAH,
BENGAL, INDIA,
1901

DEAR JOE, (Miss Josephine MacLeod.)

I can't even in imagination pay the immense debt of gratitude I owe you. Wherever you are you never forget my welfare; and, there, you are the only one that bears all my burdens, all my brutal outbursts.

Your Japanese friend has been very kind, but my health is so poor that I am rather afraid I have not much time to spare for Japan. I will drag myself through the Bombay Presidency even if only to say, "How do you do?" to all kind friends.

Then two months will be consumed in coming and going, and only one month to stay; that is not much of a chance for work, is it?

So kindly pay the money your Japanese friend has sent for my passage. I shall give it back to you when you come to India in November.

I have had a terrible collapse in Assam from which I am slowly recovering. The Bombay people have waited and waited till they are sick — must see them this time.

If in spite of all this you wish me to come, I shall start the minute you write.

I had a letter from Mrs. Leggett from London asking whether the £300 have reached me safe. They have, and I had written a week or so before to her the acknowledgment, C/o Monroe & Co., Paris, as per her previous instructions.

Her last letter came to me with the envelope ripped up in a most barefaced manner! The post offices in India don't even try to do the opening of my mail decently.

Ever yours with love,

VIVEKANANDA.

CVIII

THE MATH,
5th July, 1901.

MY DEAR MARY, (Miss Mary Hale.)

I am very thankful for your very long and nice letter, especially as I needed just such a one to cheer me up a bit. My health has been and is very bad. I recover for a few days only; then comes the inevitable collapse. Well, this is the nature of the disease anyway.

I have been touring of late in Eastern Bengal and Assam. Assam is, next to Kashmir, the most beautiful country in India, but very unhealthy. The huge Brahmaputra winding in and out of mountains and hills, studded with islands, is of course worth one's while to see.

My country is, as you know, the land of waters. But never did I realise before what that meant. The rivers of East Bengal are oceans of rolling fresh water, not rivers, and so long that steamers work on them for weeks. Miss MacLeod is in Japan. She is of course charmed with the country and asked me to come over, but my health not permitting such a long voyage, I desisted. I have seen Japan before.

So you are enjoying Venice. The old man must be delicious; only Venice was the home of old Shylock, was it not?

Sam is with you this year — I am so glad! He must be enjoying the good things of Europe after his dreary experience in the North. I have not made any interesting friends of late, and the old ones that you knew of, have nearly all passed away, even the Raja of Khetri. He died of a fall from a high tower at Secundra, the tomb of Emperor Akbar. He was repairing this old grand piece of architecture at his own expense at Agra, and one day while on inspection, he missed his footing, and it was a sheer fall of several hundred feet. Thus we sometimes come to grief on account of our zeal for antiquity. Take care, Mary, don't be too zealous for your piece of Indian antiquity.

In the Mission Seal, the snake represents mysticism; the sun knowledge; the worked up waters activity; the lotus love; the swan the soul in the midst of all.

With love to Sam and to mother,

Ever with love,

VIVEKANANDA.

PS. My letter had to be short; I am out of sorts all the time; it is the body!

CIX

THE MATH, BELUR,
6th July, 1901.

DEAR CHRISTINE,

Things come to me by fits — today I am in a fit of writing. The first thing to do is, therefore, to pen a few lines to you. I am known to be nervous, I worry much; but it seems, dear Christine, you are not far behind in that trick. One of our poets says, "Even the mountains will fly, the fire will be cold, yet the heart of the great will never change." I am small, very, but I know you are great, and my faith is always in your true heart. *I worry about everything except you.* I have dedicated you to the Mother. She is your shield, your guide. No harm can reach you — nothing hold you down a minute. I know it.

Ever yours in the Lord,

VIVEKANANDA.

CX

THE MATH, BELUR,
HOWRAH DIST., BENGAL,
27th August, 1901.

MY DEAR MARY, (Miss Mary Hale.)

I would that my health were what you expected — at least to write you a long letter. It is getting worse, in fact, every day, and so many complications and botherations without that. I have ceased to notice it at all.

I wish you all joy in your lovely Swiss chalet — splendid health, good appetite, and a light study of Swiss or other antiquities just to liven things up a bit. I am so glad you are breathing the free air of the mountains, but sorry that Sam is not in the best of health. Well, there is no anxiety about it, he has naturally such a fine physique. . . .

"Women's moods and man's luck — the gods themselves do not know, what to speak of man?" My instincts may be very feminine, but what I am exercised with just this moment is, that you get a little bit of manliness about you. Oh! Mary, your brain, health, beauty, everything is going to waste just for lack of that one essential — assertion of individuality. Your haughtiness, spirit, etc. are all nonsense, only mockery; you are at best a boarding-school girl, no backbone! no backbone!

Alas! this lifelong leading-string business! This is very harsh, very brutal; but I can't help it. I love you, Mary, sincerely, genuinely; I can't cheat you with namby-pamby sugar candies. Nor do they ever come to me.

Then again, I am a dying man; I have no time to fool in. Wake up, girl. I expect now from you letters of the right slashing order; give it right straight; I need at good deal of rousing.

I did not hear anything of the MacVeaghs when they were here. I have not had any direct message from Mrs. Bull or Niveditâ, but I hear regularly from Mrs. Sevier, and they are all in Norway as guests of Mrs. Bull.

I don't know when Nivedita comes to India or if she ever comes back.

I am in a sense a retired man; I don't keep much note of what is going on about the Movement; then the Movement is getting bigger, and it is impossible for one man to know all about it minutely.

I now do nothing, except trying to eat and sleep and nurse my body the rest of the time. Good-bye, dear Mary; hope we shall meet again somewhere in this life, but, meeting or no meeting, I remain,

Ever your loving brother,

VIVEKANANDA.

CXI

THE MATH, BELUR,
HOWRAH,
29th August, 1901.

BLESSED AND BELOVED (Shri M. N. Banerji.)

I am getting better, though still very weak. . . . The present disturbance is simply nervous. Anyhow I am getting better every day.

I am so much beholden to mother (Holy Mother — Shri Sarada Devi) for her kind proposal, only I am told by everybody in the Math that Nilambar Babu's place and the whole of the village of Belur at that becomes very malarious this month and the next. Then the rent is so extravagant. I would therefore advise mother to take a little house in Calcutta if she decides to come. I may in all probability go and live there, as it is not good for me to catch malaria over and above the present prostration. I have not asked the opinion of Saradananda or Brahmananda yet. Both are in Calcutta. Calcutta is healthier these two months and very much less expensive.

After all, let her do as she is guided by the Lord. We can only suggest and may be entirely wrong.

If she selects Nilambar's house for residence, do first arrange the rent etc. beforehand. "Mother" knows best. That is all I know too.

With all love and blessings,

Ever yours in the Lord,

VIVEKANANDA.

CXII

THE MATH, BELUR,
HOWRAH DIST.,
7th September, 1901.

BLESSED AND BELOVED, (Shri M. N. Banerji.)

I had to consult Brahmananda and others, and they were everyone in Calcutta, hence the delay in replying to your last.

The idea of taking a house for a whole year must be worked out with deliberation. As on the one hand there is some risk of catching malaria in Belur this month, in Calcutta on the other hand there is the danger of plague. Then again one is sure to avoid fever if one takes good care not to go into the interior of this village, the immediate bank of the river being entirely free from fever. Plague has not come to the river yet, and all the available places in this village are filled with Marwaris during the plague season.

Then again you ought to mention the maximum rent you can pay, and we seek the house accordingly. The quarter in the city is another suggestion. For myself, I have almost become a foreigner to Calcutta. But others will soon find a house after your mind. The sooner you decide these two points: (1) Whether mother stays at Belur or Calcutta, (2) If Calcutta, what rent and quarter, the better, as it can be done in a trice after receiving your reply.

Yours with love and blessings,

VIVEKANANDA.

PS. We are all right here. Moti has returned after his week's stay in Calcutta. It is raining here day and night last three days. Two of our cows have calved.

V.

CXIII

THE MATH, BELUR,

HOWRAH,

8th November, 1901.

MY DEAR JOE, (Miss Josephine MacLeod.)

By this this time you must have received the letter explaining the word abatement. I did not write the letter nor send the wire. I was too ill at the time to do either. I have been ever since my trip to East Bengal almost bedridden. Now I am worse than ever with the additional disadvantage of impaired eyesight. I would not write these things, but some people require details, it seems.

Well, I am so glad that you are coming over with your Japanese friends — they will have every attention in my power. I will most possibly be in Madras. I have been thinking of leaving Calcutta next week and working my way gradually to the South.

I do not know whether it will be possible to see the Orissan temples in company with your Japanese friends. I do not know whether I shall be allowed inside myself — owing to my eating "Mlechchha" food. Lord Curzon was not allowed inside.

However, your friends are welcome to what I can do always. Miss Müller is in Calcutta. Of course she has not visited us.

Yours with all love,

VIVEKANANDA.

CXIV

GOPAL LAL VILLA,
BENARES (VARANASI) CANTONMENT,
9th February, 1902.

MY DEAR SWARUP(ÂNANDA),

. . . In answer to Châru's letter, tell him to study the *Brahma-Sutras* himself. What does he mean by the *Brahma-Sutras* containing references to Buddhism? He means the Bhâshyas, of course, or rather ought to mean, and Shankara was only the last Bhâshyakâra (commentator). There are references, though in Buddhistic literature, to Vedanta, and the Mahâyâna school of Buddhism is even Advaitistic. Why does Amara Singha, a Buddhist, give as one of the names of Buddha — Advayavâdi ? Charu writes, the word Brahman does not occur in the Upanishads! *Quelle bêtise*!

I hold the Mahayana to be the older of the two schools of Buddhism.

The theory of Mâyâ is as old as the Rik-Samhitâ. The Shvetâshvatara Upanishad contains the word "Maya" which is developed out of Prakriti. I hold that Upanishad to be at least older than Buddhism.

I have had much light of late about Buddhism, and I am ready to prove:

(1) That Shiva-worship, in various forms, antedated the Buddhists, that the Buddhists tried to get hold of the sacred places of the Shaivas but, failing in that, made new places in the precincts just as you find now at Bodh-Gayâ and Sârnâth (Varanasi).

(2) The story in the Agni Purâna about Gayâsura does not refer to Buddha at all — as Dr. Rajendralal will have it — but simply to a pre-existing story.

(3) That Buddha went to live on Gayâshirsha mountain proves the pre-existence of the place.

(4) Gaya was a place of ancestor-worship already, and the footprint-worship the Buddhists copied from the Hindus.

(5) About Varanasi, even the oldest records go to prove it as the great place of Shiva-worship; etc., etc.

Many are the new facts I have gathered in Bodh-Gaya and from Buddhist literature. Tell Charu to read for himself, and not be swayed by foolish opinions.

I am rather well here, in Varanasi, and if I go on improving in this way, it will be a great gain.

A total revolution has occurred in my mind about the relation of Buddhism and Neo-Hinduism. I may not live to work out the glimpses, but I shall leave the lines of work indicated, and you and your brethren will have to work it out.

Yours with all blessings and love,

VIVEKANANDA.

CXV

GOPAL LAL VILLA,
BENARES (VARANASI) CANTONMENT,
10th February, 1902.

Welcome to India once more, dear mother (Mrs. Ole Bull) and daughter. A copy of a Madras journal that I received through the kindness of Joe delighted me exceedingly, as the reception Niveditâ had in Madras was for the good of both Nivedita and Madras. Her speech was indeed beautiful.

I hope you are resting well after your long journey, and so is Nivedita. I wish it so much that you should go for a few hours to a few villages west of Calcutta to see the old Bengali structures made of wood, bamboo, cane, mica, and grass.

These are the bungalows, most artistic. Alas! the name is travestied nowadays by every pigsty appropriating the name.

In old days a man who built a palace still built a bungalow for the reception of guests. The art is dying out. I wish I could build the whole of Nivedita's School in that style. Yet it is good to see the few that yet remained, at least one.

Brahmananda will arrange for it, and you have only to take a journey of a few hours.

Mr. Okakura has started on his short tour. He intends to visit Agra, Gwalior, Ajanta, Ellora, Chittore, Udaipur, Jaipur, and Delhi.

A very well-educated rich young man of Varanasi, with whose father we had a long-standing friendship, came back to this city yesterday. He is especially interested in art, and spending purposely a lot of money in his attempts to revive dying Indian arts. He came to see me only a few hours after Mr. Okakura left. He is just the man to show him artistic India (i.e. what little is left), and I am sure he will be much benefited by Okakura's suggestions. Okakura just found a common terracotta water-vessel here used by the servants. The shape and the embossed work on it simply charmed him, but as it is common earthenware and would not bear the journey, he left a request with me to have it reproduced in brass. I was at my wit's end as to what to do. My young friend comes a few hours after, and not only undertakes to have it done but offers to show a few hundreds of embossed designs in terracotta infinitely superior to the one Okakura fancied.

He also offers to show us old paintings in that wonderful old style. Only one family is left in Varanasi who can paint after the old style yet. One of them has painted a whole hunting scene on a pea, perfect in detail and action!

I hope Okakura will come to this city on his return and be this gentleman's guest and see a bit of what is left.

Niranjan has gone with Mr. Okakura, and as he is a Japanese, they don't object to his going into any temple. It seems that the Tibetans and the other Northern Buddhists have been coming here to worship Shiva all along.

They allowed him to touch the sign of Shiva and worship. Mrs. Annie Besant tried once, but, poor woman, although she bared her feet, put on a Sari, and humiliated herself to the dust before the priests, she was not admitted even into the compound of the temple. The Buddhists are not considered non-Hindus in any of our great temples. My plans are not settled; I may shift from this place very soon.

Shivananda and the boys send you all their welcome, regards, and love.

I am, as ever, your most affectionate son

VIVEKANANDA.

CXVI

BENARES (VARANASI),
12th February, 1902.

May all powers come unto you! (Sister Nivedita) May Mother Herself be your hands and mind! It is immense power — irresistible — that I pray for you, and, if possible, along with it infinite peace. . . .

If there was any truth in Shri Ramakrishna, may He take you into His leading, even as He did me, nay, a thousand times more!

VIVEKANANDA.

CXVII

(Translated from Bengali)

GOPAL LAL VILLA,
BENARES (VARANASI) CANTONMENT,
12th February 1902.

MY DEAR RAKHAL, (Swami Brahmananda.)

I was glad to get all the detailed news from your letter. Regarding Nivedita's School, I have written to her what I have to say. My opinion is that she should do what she considers to be best.

Don't ask my opinion on any other matter either. That makes me lose my temper. Just do that work for me — that is all. Send money, for at present only a few rupees are left.

Kanai (Nirbhayananda) lives on Mâdhukari (Cooked food obtained by begging from several houses.), does his Japa at the bathing ghat, and comes and sleeps here at night; Nyedâ does a poor man's work and comes and sleeps here at night. "Uncle" and Niranjan have gone to Agra. I may get their letter today.

Continue doing your work as the Lord guides. Why bother about the opinion of this man and that? My love to all.

Yours affectionately.

VIVEKANANDA.

CXVIII

(Translated from Bengali)

GOPAL LAL VILLA,
BENARES (VARANASI) CANTONMENT,
18th February, 1902.

MY DEAR RAKHAL, (Swami Brahmananda.)

You must have received by this time my letter of yesterday containing an acknowledgment of the money. The main object of this letter is to write about — —. You should go and meet him as soon as you get this letter. . . . Get a competent doctor and have the disease diagnosed properly. Now where is Vishnu Mohini, the eldest daughter of Ram Babu (Ram Chandra Datta, a disciple of Shri Ramakrishna)? She has recently been widowed. . . .

Anxiety is worse than the disease. Give a little money — whatever is needed. If in this hell of a world one can bring a little joy and peace even for a day into the heart of a single person, that much alone is true; this I have learnt after suffering all my life; all else is mere moonshine. . . .

Reply very soon. "Uncle" (Mr. Okakura was emdearingly so called. "Kura" approximating to "Khurhâ" in Bengali which means uncle; Swamiji out of fun calls him uncle.) and Niranjan have written a letter from Gwalior. . . Here it is now becoming hot gradually. This place was cooler than Bodh-Gaya. . . . I was very pleased to hear that the Saraswati-Puja was celebrated by Nivedita with great success. If she wants to open the school soon, let her do so. Readings from the sacred books, worship, study — see that all these are being maintained. My love to all.

Yours affectionately,

VIVEKANANDA.

CXIX

(Translated from Bengali)

GOPAL LAL VILLA,
BENARES (VARANASI) CANTONMENT,
21st February, 1902.

MY DEAR RAKHAL,

I received a letter from you just now. If mother and grandmother desire to come, send them over. It is better to get away from Calcutta now when the season of plague is on. There is wide-spread plague in Allahabad; I do not know if it will spread to Varanasi this time . . . . Tell Mrs. Bull from me that a tour to Ellora and other places involves a difficult journey, and it is now very hot. Her body is so tired that it is not proper to go on a tour at present. It is several days since I received a letter from "Uncle" (Mr. Okakura was endearingly so called. "Kura" approximating to "Khurhâ" in Bengali which means uncle; Swamiji out of fun calls him uncle.). The last news was that he had gone to Ajanta. Mahant also has not replied, perhaps he will do so with the reply to Raja Pyari Mohan's letter. . . .

Write me in detail about the matter of the Nepal Minister. Give my special love and blessings to Mrs. Bull, Miss MacLeod, and all others. My love and greetings to you, Baburam (Swami Premananda), and all others. Has Gopal Dada (Swami Advaitananda) got the letter? Kindly look after the goat a bit.

Yours affectionately,

VIVEKANANDA.

PS. All the boys here send you their respectful salutations.

CXX

(Translated from Bengali)

GOPAL LAL VILLA,
BENARES (VARANASI) CANTONMENT,
24th February, 1902.

This morning I got a small American parcel sent by you. (Swami Brahmananda) I have received no letter, neither the registered one you refer to nor any other. Whether the Nepalese gentleman came and what happened — I have not been able to know anything at all about it. To write a simple letter so much trouble and so much delay! . . . Now I shall be relieved if I get the accounts. That also I get who knows after how many months! . . .

Yours affectionately,

VIVEKANANDA.

CXXI

THE MATH
21st April, 1902

DEAR JOE, (Miss Josephine MacLeod.)

It seems the plan of going to Japan seems to have come to nought Mrs. Bull is gone, you are going. I am not sufficiently acquainted with th Japanese.

Sadananda has accompanied the Japanese to Nepal along with Kanai Christine could not start earlier, as Margot could not go till the end of thi month.

I am getting on splendidly, they say, but yet very weak and no wate to drink. Anyhow the chemical analysis shows a great improvement. Th swelling about the feet and the complaints have all disappeared.

Give my infinite love to Lady Betty and Mr. Leggett, to Alberta an Holly — the baby has my blessings from before birth and will have for eve

How did you like Mayavati? Write me a line about it.

With everlasting lov

VIVEKANAND

CXXII

THE MATH,
BELUR, HOWRAH,
15th May, 1902.

DEAR JOE, (Miss Josephine MacLeod.)

I send you the letter to Madame Calvé.

. . .

I am somewhat better, but of course far from what I expected. A great idea of quiet has come upon me. I am going to retire for good — no more work for me. If possible, I will revert to my old days of begging.

All blessings attend you, Joe; you have been a good angel to me.

With everlasting love,
VIVEKANANDA.

CXXIII

THE MATH,
14th June, 1902.

DEAR DHIRÂ MÂTÂ, (Mrs. Ole Bull.)

. . . In my opinion, a race must first cultivate a great respect for motherhood, through the sanctification and inviolability of marriage, before it can attain to the ideal of perfect chastity. The Roman Catholics and the Hindus, holding marriage sacred and inviolate, have produced great chaste men and women of immense power. To the Arab, marriage is a contrac or a forceful possession, to be dissolved at will, and we do not find there the development of the idea of the virgin or the Brahmachârin. Modern Buddhism — having fallen among races who had not yet come up to the evolution of marriage — has made a travesty of monasticism. So until there is developed in Japan a great and sacred ideal about marriage (apart from mutual attraction and love), I do not see how there can be great monks and nuns. As you have come to see that the glory of life is chastity, so my eye also have been opened to the necessity of this great sanctification for th vast majority, in order that a few lifelong chaste powers may be produced . . .

I wanted to write many things, but the flesh is weak . . . "Whosoeve worships me, for whatsoever desire, I meet him with that." . . .

VIVEKANAND.